From Pictures to Words

From Pictures to Words

a guide to choosing books for beginner readers

PATRICIA FITZGERALD

Clare County Library

CLARE COUNTY LIBRARY HEADQUARTERS
Mill Road, Ennis, Co. Clare

© Clare County Library 2004

ISBN 0-9541870-1-6

Book Selection & Reviews by Patricia Fitzgerald & Anne Finnucane

Design & Layout Ed Butler

Cover & Artwork © Domingo Cuatindioy 2004

Printed by Colour Books, Dublin

Introduction

It is the policy of Clare County Library to actively promote the reading habit, not being content to just stack books on shelves. This reading promotion is important for young people, particularly for those children who are beginning to read on their own.

Patricia Fitzgerald, Librarian, Children's Services, ensures that our young people are not forgotten and through publications such as this, are provided with advice on choosing suitable reading material. Her first book *Picture This: A Guide to Choosing Books for Young Children*, recommending books for young children was highly successful and continues to prove very valuable to parents and teachers.

Now comes the next volume, *From Pictures to Words: A Guide to Choosing Books for Beginner Readers*. This book is aimed at children who are beginning to read on their own as well as more confident readers. The stories selected include some classics and a selection of short novels, featuring fewer illustrations and longer sentences for the more confident reader and a range of what are often described as "chapter" books.

It is important that the books children are presented with at a stage when they are making the transition from picture books to first readers will inspire continued reading and a progression to a life long love of books. We hope to work towards this objective with the selection of books in this guide.

This publication is invaluable not just to parents and teachers but to everyone with an interest in books and reading, not least the children themselves. Books in the Irish language are also included with a separate section devoted to recommended titles.

In a new departure for Clare County Library, a series of works by Colombian artist Domingo Cuatindioy, have been commissioned to illustrate the book. Based between Lahinch and the Colombian Andes, Domingo's evocative style appeals to adults and children alike and brings a magical element to this book which will fire any child's imagination.

Our gratitude is also due to Anne Finnucane, Senior Library Assistant, Sweeney Memorial Library, Kilkee for her assistance in selecting and reviewing titles. Thanks also to Maureen Comber, Executive Librarian and Siobhan Mulcahy, Clare County Arts Officer for their advice and assistance with this publication.
We would also like to thank Conor Keane and his team at An Clár as Gaeilge for their help with translation.

Noel Crowley,
County Librarian.

Other Animal Poems   The Cat in the Hat   Puppy and the Sausage   Boom Chicka Boo

Dirty Gertie Mackintosh Skyscraper Ted and Other Zany Verse Worms Can't Fly Bad Bad Cats Jungle Jingles &

Dirty Gertie Mackintosh   Skyscraper Ted and Other Zany Verse   Worms Can't Fly

RHYME

Bad Bad Cats Jungle Jingles & Other Animal Poems The Cat in the Hat Puppy and the Sausage Boom Chicka Boom

Published by Corgi, 1997
ISBN 0-552-52800-5
Illustrations © Ros Asquith, 1996

Dirty Gertie Mackintosh by Dick King-Smith

"Washed your hands?" her mum would cry.
" 'Course I have," she would reply.
"But it always was a lie".

These three lines, taken from Dick King Smith's collection of poems entitled *Dirty Gertie Mackintosh*, sum up Gertie's hygiene habits – or rather the lack of them. When it gets to the point where her friends can no longer tolerate "the smelly little fool" they decide to chuck her in the swimming pool and will only pull her out when she promises to wash "for all eternity".

The first poem in *Dirty Gertie Mackintosh* sets the tone for the other fourteen to follow. Gertie is just one of an array of eccentric characters whose exploits will cause children to laugh out loud. There's Miss Emily Berry – the strongest girl in the school – Arthur Best who sets off to climb Mount Everest, and Fred Moon, whose extraordinary big ears become the envy of almost every single kid in England. With a vocabulary simple enough for beginner readers and plenty of illustration, it's an ideal introduction to verse with an ample helping of good fun as well.

Worms Can't Fly by Aislinn & Larry O'Loughlin

If you would like to read poems about two-headed aliens, dogs with no noses, or an eighty-three year old roller-blading granny, then this book of poems is for you. Children are often reluctant to read poetry but, presented with this hilarious, quirky selection, they should soon change their minds.
Here's a taste of what's in store, taken from a poem entitled "Mum".

Mum, make her give my roller-blades back
She's had them most of the day
and tell her to grow up and act her age –
after all, Granny is eighty-three

Published by Wolfhound Press, 2000
ISBN 0-86327-786-1

Bad Bad Cats by Roger McGough

Divided into three sections – The Cats' Protection League, Waxing Lyrical and Carnival of the Animals – this wonderfully witty collection from Roger McGough contains a total of seventy-six poems in all. The first five poems feature the gangster cats; the bad bad cats of the title.

An interesting mixture of rhyming and non-rhyming verse is supplemented with what are simply lists of helpful hints for people like new teachers, who should never swap confiscated Beano comics for the P.E. teacher's bubble gum; scuba divers, who are advised to practise at home in the bath before diving into shark-infested waters; and travellers to whom it's suggested that destinations are ideal places to head for!

Published by The Penguin Group, 1997
ISBN 0-140-38391-3
Illustrations © Lydia Monks, 1997

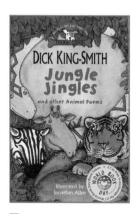

Published by Young Corgi, 2002
ISBN 0-552-54835-9
Illustrations © Jonathan Allen, 2002

Jungle Jingles and Other Animal Poems by Dick King-Smith

This edition of *Jungle Jingles* was published specially for World Book Day 2002. Written by best-selling children's author Dick King-Smith, there is no shortage of information on animals from pigmy shrews to hippos.

Find out why the dromedary always has a hump; what to do if an earwig gets inside your ear; or why giraffes can be lost for words.

"This joyfully funny collection begs to be read aloud to young children."
The Times Educational Supplement

3

Puppy and the Sausage by Gabriel Fitzmaurice

A collection of poems for children of all ages, including adults, is how this book is described on the back cover. One of the **Poolbeg Wren** series, it is suited for reading aloud with a child or for more confident readers to enjoy alone.
A large variety of poems about family life are interspersed with very funny poems about everyday happenings.

"Daddy's Belly", "Nora" and "A Goodnight Kiss" are three with a distinctive Irish ring to them.
"I'm the Horse's Bum in the Panto", "Smelly Socks and Hairy Legs" and "I'd Like To Be" are examples of the poet's exact interpretation of child humour.

Published by Poolbeg Press Ltd., 1998
ISBN 1-85371-858-0
Illustrations © Stewart Curry, 1998

Boom Chicka Boom by Liz Weir

This is a wonderful collection of poetry, stories and action rhymes from one of Ireland's best known storytellers, Liz Weir. "Going to Granny's", the first story in the collection, is introduced by the author as a participation story for everyone to join in.

Children are invited to help pack Susie's case, get settled in for the night and choose her companions. With lots of repetition, and instructions from Liz on how to provide the sound effects, the story comes to life and is typical of the remaining stories and poems to follow.

The author's energy and zest exude through her writing with each poem, action rhyme or story coming alive to enthral young readers.
The book works equally well for 6 to 8 year olds to read themselves, or alternatively, it is an ideal read-aloud for pre-schoolers.

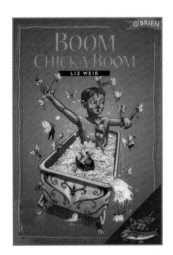

Published by The O'Brien Press Ltd., 1995
ISBN 0-86278-417-4

Published by HarperCollins Ltd., 1997
ISBN 0-00-171303-5

The Cat in the Hat by Dr. Seuss

Dr. Seuss' books are traditionally acclaimed as learning-to-read books. Simple to read, zany stories, silly rhymes and crazy drawings combine to endear the whole range to children. The Cat in the Hat character offers lots of "good fun that is funny" to Sally and her brother whose boredom the reader can almost feel in Dr. Seuss' description in the opening rhyming lines of the story.

Complete chaos takes over in the house while mother's out despite the warnings of the Fish in the Pot! The trademark red and blue colours of Dr. Seuss' books carried throughout the whole story add to children's sense of familiarity with all books in the series.

Skyscraper Ted and Other Zany Verse by Margot Bosonnet

A total of forty-seven poems make up this collection of poetry for children, described at the time of publishing by the Evening Press as "one of the best Irish collections of children's verse in a long time." While poems like "Mr. Potts goes Bananas", proclaiming the merits of wearing bananas on your head, or "Dangerous Waters", telling of the perils of unwanted baths, will strike a chord with young children, other poems in the collection may need a little adult explanation.

The wide range of material covered will introduce children to playing with words and the idea of fun through poetry. Comic black and white drawings accompany almost every poem.

Published by Wolfhound Press, 1994
ISBN 0-86327-406-4
Illustrations © Wolfhound Press

children's
classics

children's
classics

Published by Mammoth, 1991
ISBN 0-7497-0723-2

The Little Prince by Antoine de Saint-Exupéry

After having to make a forced landing in the Sahara desert the author meets the Little Prince. Little by little, and only from answers gleaned by chance, does he come to learn where the Little Prince has come from.

Through their encounter, Antoine de Saint Exupéry shows us the folly of our ways as humans. The story takes the form of a parable that could be appreciated just as much by adults as by children, and both will enjoy the author's superb illustrations.

Visiting the neighbouring asteroids the Little Prince meets many interesting characters, including a king who has no subjects, a conceited man, and a train operator who re-routes trains full of people who don't know where they're going or why. Only the children enjoy the trip.

The Little Prince is a book for advanced readers but is also an ideal book for sharing with younger children. There is no end to the opportunity for discussion that a book like this can inspire.

My Naughty Little Sister by Dorothy Edwards

This classic tale of the author's very naughty little sister has delighted its readers for over fifty years. Children will enjoy the mischievous behaviour of the naughtiest little girl in the world, and the outrage of her older sister at her pursuits.

Each of the fifteen chapters in the book is a self-contained story written in a very simple style, covering just six or seven pages in large type. It is an ideal beginner reader for young children.

Published by Mammoth, 1998
ISBN 0-7497-0054-8
Illustrations © Shirley Hughes, 1962

The Hundred and One Dalmatians by Dodie Smith

First published in 1956, *The Hundred and One Dalmatians* became the basis for the smash hit Disney movie of the same name.

The story is told from the dogs' viewpoint. Pongo and Missis find it touching that their humans actually believe they own the dogs, instead of realising that they, the dogs, own them.

Cruella De Vil is a very evil woman. She will do anything to have a dalmatian fur coat. She is determined to turn the adorable dalmatian puppies born to Pongo and Missis into just that. Having set about buying all the dalmatians she can find, her plan is foiled when the Dearlys refuse to sell their much loved pets. But with the help of Saul and Jasper Baddun she succeeds in her mission and, one cold windy day, all the dalmatian puppies disappear.

Enlisting the help of their friends through The Twilight Bark, Pongo and Missis are reunited not only with their own family but with all the other dalmatians that Cruella and her team have stolen. Their adventures along the way continue to delight children of the twenty-first century, just as they did when the book was first written in 1956. This is a must for all dog lovers, young and old.

Published by Heinemann, 1993
ISBN 0-434-96066-7
Illustrations © Vanessa Julian-Ottie, 1993

The Wind in the Willows by Kenneth Grahame

The reader's attention is engaged from the very beginning of *The Wind in the Willows*. The well-loved story of Ratty, Badger, Mole and Toad and their adventures on the river bank and in the wild wood, make this a classic to keep, read and read again over the years.

Children will relate to many of Mole's personality traits including his boastfulness, his greed, and his lack of apprehension when trying out anything new.

A total of 242 pages in this edition make for quite a long story. Children of this age might be glad to have some chapters read to them. Having the story read aloud should also help to keep their interest which might otherwise wane in a story of this length.

Published by The Penguin Group, 1994
ISBN 0-14-036685-7
Illustrations © Robin Lawrie, 1994

Little The Hundred & One Dalmations The Wind in the Willows Matilda The Wizard of Oz Peter Pan Stig

Published by The Penguin Group, 2001
ISBN 0-14-131136-3
Illustrations © Quentin Blake, 1988

Matilda by Roald Dahl

Matilda is a truly extraordinary girl. She lives with her family but they look on her as a pest, someone who is more trouble than she is worth. Neither her father, Mr Wormwood – the crooked car dealer whose main pleasure in life is watching telly – or her mother, who is hooked on playing bingo every afternoon, have any time for books. Books are Matilda's reason for being.

When Matilda starts school she makes friends for the first time in her life. She loves Miss Honey, her teacher, but Miss Trunchbull, the school principal, hates children and is horrible to all of them. Matilda decides to use her extraordinary gift to help Miss Honey get back her house and money from Miss Trunchbull.

The story of Matilda and her teacher, their hard childhoods and their triumph over their bullying, uncaring families is a real Roald Dahl classic and is both a sad and funny read.

The Wizard of Oz by L. Frank Baum

The story of Dorothy and her little dog Toto is a well known classic adventure which inspired the film now as famous as the book itself. The book is written in an easy style despite it's being quite a long story.

When a cyclone hits Dorothy's home in Kansas she and her dog are whisked away to a magical land from which she must follow the yellow brick road to lead her home. Her journey introduces us to the many strange companions she meets, like the Tin Woodman, Scarecrow and the Cowardly Lion and the problems that they themselves feel they have.

Published by The Penguin Group, 1994
ISBN 0-14-036693-8
Illustrations © David McKee, 1982

There is plenty food for discussion and thought for readers of all ages often concealed under a humourous surface with a sense of adventure that carries the reader along.

The audience with the wonderful wizard turns out to be a non-event, the wizard himself proving to be nothing more than a humbug. In the same chapter we are indirectly advised to look inside ourselves for the human qualities of courage, kindness and intellect. The futility of searching for them is underlined in the Lion's search for courage, the Tin Woodman's search for a heart and the Scarecrow's search for brains.

Depending on the reader's interpretation, *The Wizard of Oz* can be a simple adventure story or a documentary on our perceptions of what's important in life.

Peter Pan by J.M Barrie

This is a magical tale of Peter Pan – the young boy who will never grow old – and of his adventures in Neverland with the Darling children Wendy, Michael and John. The Darlings live in London with their parents and nanny, a Newfoundland dog. Their father is extremely proper and works in stocks and shares. He likes things to look proper and gets very upset if they're not just so. Their mother, who first discovered Peter Pan as she was tidying her children's minds at bedtime, (as all good mothers do!), is a lovely lady with a romantic mind and a sweet mocking mouth.

As *Peter Pan* was first written in 1904 by J. M. Barrie, the language is somewhat old- world, but it has lost none of its magic and still continues to fascinate its readers. It is a wonderful story suited for older children or for parents to select as a bedtime read.

Published by The Penguin Group, 1994
ISBN 0-14-036674-1
Illustrations © Elisa Trimby, 1986

Published by Viking Kestrel, 1980
ISBN 0-670-80027-9
Illustrations © Edward Ardizzone, 1963

Stig of the Dump by Clive King

Stig of the Dump is a series of funny and exciting adventures that begin with Barney's plummet into the chalk-pit in the dump. Straying near the chalk-pit was the thing he was most warned against but, of course, it was the thing he most wanted to do.

The suspense generated in the opening chapter will make reading the whole book an absolute must. The fact that Stig the cave man wears only rabbit skins and speaks only in grunts doesn't matter to Barney, underlining the ability of children to communicate without words.

His sister and grandmother think Stig is purely a figment of Barney's imagination. Barney does nothing to convince them of the truth, knowing he will be left in peace to share several adventures with his friend. These adventures culminate in a trip back in time to share in Stig's tribal party.

First published in 1963, this children's classic will be enjoyed for its sense of excitement and adventure and for its commentary on true friendship as much today as it was then.

Little The Hundred & One Dalmations The Wind in the Willows Matilda The Wizard of Oz Peter Pan Stig

Published by The Penguin Group, 1994
ISBN 0-14-036666-0
Illustrations © Robin Lawrie, 1994

The Secret Garden by Frances Hodgson Burnett

Mary Lennox is a spoiled, self-centred child. Her parents die in India of cholera and Mary is the only survivor in the house. Her mother and father were preoccupied with their own lives and never showed her any love. The only one who cared for her was her nurse or Ayah, but she also died in the cholera epidemic.

Mary moves home to England to be brought up by her uncle, whom she has never met. She discovers she has a cousin, Colin, a sickly child, abandoned to the care of the housekeeper of Misselthwaite Manor. She also discovers that her new home in England is not a happy one.

Mary soon discovers a walled garden neglected and overgrown. With the help of Dickon, the servant boy, and Colin, they bring the garden back to its former beauty and in doing so, heal their own hearts and souls.

Charlotte's Web by E.B. White

The story of Wilbur the pig and his good friend Charlotte the grey spider is set in America. When Wilbur is born, he is the runt of the litter and eight-year-old Fern Arable saves him from death. She cares for him until he is two months old and then he goes to her uncle's farm. At the farm Wilbur meets his best and only friend Charlotte, and she devises a clever plan to save him from slaughter.

This is a powerful story of love and enduring friendship and is a treasured classic. The book is complemented by the lovely illustrations of Garth Williams. *Charlotte's Web* was first published in 1952 and is a timeless story that will be enjoyed by children for many years to come.

Published by The Penguin Group, 1993
ISBN 0-14-036449-8

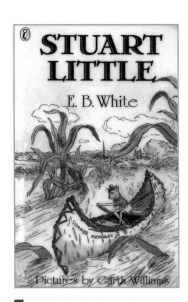

Published by The Penguin Group, 2000
ISBN 0-14-130506-1
Illustrations © Garth Williams, 1973

Stuart Little by E.B. White

The hit film *Stuart Little* has brought the book by the same name, first published in the U.S.A. in 1945, to the attention of millions of children worldwide. This edition, published in 2000, is greatly enhanced by the pictures of Garth Williams and makes a great read for children and adults alike.

Stuart Little is no ordinary mouse. Only two inches tall he survives in a world of adult humans with the added hazard of sharing his home with Snowbell the cat, in the heart of New York city. The story of Stuart Little is just one adventure after another, and when his adventures turn out to be dangerous, he gets absolutely no help from Snowbell, who delights in seeing him in trouble.

Stuart Little introduces the themes of friendship and families, each chapter bringing a new adventure which will help sustain the interest of young readers.

sports
& pastimes

sports
      & pastimes

Sports Day for Charlie by Joy Allen

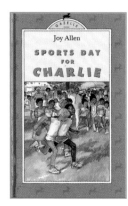

Charlie bans all sorts of fattening foods in an effort to rid Dad of his big tummy before Sports Day. Hearing that Charlie's friends say he is too unfit to run is just the incentive Dad needs to embark on a fitness campaign with Charlie as his trainer. Training begins at six o'clock each morning.

Reading very much like a precursor to the Harry Potter books, the school is divided into three Houses; Slugs, Beetles and Spiders all competing to win the Cup. Charlie and his dad triumph in the end. Charlie's House – Slugs – wins the cup and Dad crosses the line in a sporting finish, neck and neck with boastful Jake's Dad.

Divided into just three chapters, the story gently eases young readers into the concept of introduction, middle and conclusion common to all stories. Clear large type combined with black and white illustrations help children make the transition from picture books to first story books like this one very easy.

Published by The Penguin Group, 1990
ISBN 0-241-12904 – 4
Illustrations © Michael Charlton, 1990

There's Only One Danny Ogle by Helena Pielichaty

Danny is football crazy. He and his family have just moved from the town to the country and Danny is very unhappy as there is no football at Westhorpe Primary School. His enthusiasm is catching and, with the principal's permission, a team is formed.

This is a story with many different themes. The main subject of football is intertwined with social issues such as changing schools, making new friends and new beginnings. Written from nine year old Danny's very witty viewpoint it is a highly amusing read.

Published by Oxford University Press, 2001
ISBN 0-192-75121-2

Louisa's Secret by Adèle Geras

Louisa's dream is to become a ballet dancer. She goes to great pains to take care of her legs and feet, even going so far as to stop kicking her sister under the table when she calls her Weezer.

When her new neighbour and friend, a boy aged eight named Tony, moves in next door Louisa gradually encourages him to practise ballet with her. So when Miss Matting, the ballet teacher, asks everyone in her class to prepare a dance with a partner, Louisa plans to make Tony her partner. But she must keep this a secret, even from her best friends, Maisie and Tricia.

She even has to keep it a secret from Tony because he refuses to let anyone know he likes ballet. Only by pretending they're entering a talent contest does she get him to agree to dance with her. When he finally agrees to perform in front of Louisa's class he is surprised to find out that James Williams, a boy from his school is one of those "girly wimps" who do ballet. This is Book Two in the **Little Swan Ballet Books** series published by Red Fox. Other titles in the series include *Little Swan*; *Louisa in the Wings* and *Louisa and Phoebe*.

Published by Red Fox, 1997
ISBN 0-09-921832-1
Illustrations © Karen Popham, 1997

Sheltie Rides to Win by Peter Clover

Emma and her friend Sally from the Saddleback Club enter the First Little Applewoods Pony Show. However, they have stiff opposition from Simon and Alice. Will the Saddlebacks win the show or will Alice, Simon and his sister Melody win the prize? The **Sheltie** series of books are easy readers and are suited for children who can read longer stories alone. They are particularly appealing to girls who are interested in horses and horse riding.

Published by The Penguin Group, 1998
ISBN 0-14-038950-4

Soccer Mad by Rob Childs

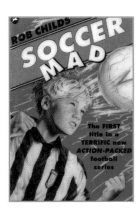

Luke is soccer mad. He is captain of the Swillsby Swifts, a Sunday League team for local village boys. All the team members are like Luke – boys who never get a look-in in their school team, but who all want to play. When the Swifts are drawn to play the Panthers in the first round of the League Cup, Luke looks forward to the challenge, but the rest of his team mates think he is being too optimistic and that they haven't a hope.

Will the teamwork, practice and tactics of the Swifts pay off in the end, or will the Panthers get the upper hand as usual? This is a book on football but even the football illiterate will enjoy it as it is a story which is full of humour and action. It is the first book in the **Big Match** series by Rob Childs.

Published by Corgi Yearling, 1996
ISBN 0-440-86344-9
Illustrations © Aidan Potts, 1996

Bad Boyz: Kicking Off by Alan Durant

"The magnificent seven" were always in detention and their teacher Mr. Davies was tired of seeing them, day after day, being punished for the same crimes. In fact, putting them on detention had no effect on their subsequent behaviour whatsoever.

One day he suggests that they make up a seven-a-side Little League Soccer Team, and offers to coach them. The children are really interested in the idea, but will Mr. Davies be able to whip the bad boyz into shape and keep them out of trouble?

This is the first book in the **Bad Boyz** series by Alan Durant. Other titles are *Leagues Apart; K.O. Kings* and *Barmy Army*. The books will go down a treat with all young soccer enthusiasts, and are made all the more enjoyable with the addition of lots of boys' cheeky humour throughout.

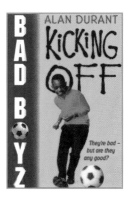

Published by Walker Books Ltd., 2001
ISBN 0-7445-5973-1

magic

magic,
witches
& wizardry

witches

& wizardry

Published by The Penguin Group, 1995
ISBN 0-14-037530-9
Illustrations © Jo Davies, 1985

Harry's Aunt by Sheila Lavelle

Attractive colour illustrations and well-spaced, simple text characteristic of the **First Young Puffin** series help children make the transition from picture books to chapter books.
Harry's Aunt by Sheila Lavelle is an ideal book for confident young readers. While holidaying with Aunt Winnie, Harry discovers she is, in fact, a witch who can turn herself into any animal where and whenever she wants. Harry gets fed up with her antics when she has to be freed from the bus after turning herself into an elephant or when, changed into a crocodile, she scares all the post-office customers on to the street.

Harry tries to keep Aunt Winnie at home but doesn't succeed when it comes to the Dog Show in the Village Hall. Read what really happens when Harry takes home a black cat presuming it's Aunt Winnie in yet another of her transformations.

The Witches by Roald Dahl

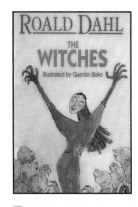

When the narrator's parents die in a car crash in the opening pages of the book, he goes to live with his Norweigan, cigar-smoking aunt. They both hatch a plan to outwit the witches, offering many helpful hints to all children at risk throughout the story.

These seemingly ordinary women in ordinary, everyday lives spend their entire existence plotting to rid their territory of children.

This is not a book for the faint hearted. Roald Dahl does not mince words in his portrayal of witches and how they work to achieve their sole aim in life. Young readers will no doubt agree with the narrator's advice that they should have a bath only once a month at the very most, because it's far easier for a witch to smell a clean child than a dirty one.

Written in that conversational style best exemplified by Roald Dahl, children will feel the author is speaking to them personally.

Published by The Penguin Group, 1985
ISBN 0-14-031730-9
Illustrations © Quentin Blake, 1983

Broomstick Removals by Anne Jungman

Published by Scholastic Ltd., 1997
ISBN 0-439-01136-1
Illustrations © Jan Lewis, 1997

Broomstick Removals is an ideal read for Halloween. It's full of action, entertainment and good fun and guaranteed to appeal to children who are beginning to read their own stories.

A fast food delivery service by broomstick isn't exactly normal. Neither is a rubbish disposal business run by witches.

Mabel is horrified when her sister Ethel promises to help the distressed Mr. Botch sort out his builder's yard. And trouble is only beginning when they both have to be up at five a.m. to clear away piles of stinky rubbish.

Things go from bad to worse when the witches' broomsticks are stolen and their original business, Broomstick Services, is sabotaged. But retired witch and "married human" sister Maud makes up her mind it's time to take out her black witch's dress again and consult her book of spells at the section marked REVENGE.

You can read the further adventures of Ethel, Mabel and Maud in *Broomstick Services*, *Broomstick Rescues* and *Broomstick Baby*.

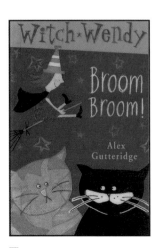

Published by MacMillan Children's Books Ltd., 2002
ISBN 0-330-39851-2
Illustrations © Annabel Hudson, 2002

Broom Broom! by Alex Gutteridge

Witch Wendy's broomstick is in the garage for repairs and she desperately needs it to take part in the Witches' Annual Broomstick Race. With her cat Snowflake's help she may just take part after all, but will her rivals Rosemary, Harriet and Primrose ever be nice to her?

Two other stories, *Cats and Hats* and *Cat Tricks* make up this easy to read series for beginners. The division of large print text into short chapters accompanied by lots of illustration is just what children aged seven or eight need to encourage independent reading.

The Witch's Dog by Stephanie Dagg

Cackling Carol must be the only witch in the world who has a dog ride on her broomstick with her instead of a cat. Cackling Carol hates cats. When she receives a message from Witch Matilda warning that the evil Wizard Egbert is in the area, Big Roddy – the biggest, shaggiest dog found by Cackling Carol in the dog's home – goes on full alert. Cackling Carol is furious when the other witches in her coven find her dog hilarious.

When Wizard Egbert turns up at the meeting disguised as a rat, with a mission to change all the witches' spell books into floppy disks – (witches were not very good with new technology) – Roddy is immune to the cat-sleeping spell Egbert weaves, and saves the day.

Stephanie Dagg writes for children of all ages. *The Witch's Dog* is ideally suited to beginner readers, as are the other books in the series, *De-Witched* and *Witching Again*.

Published by Mentor Books, 1998
ISBN 1-902586-00-X

The W-Files by Don Conroy

Artist, wildlife expert and T.V. personality, Don Conroy needs no introduction to Irish children. In *The W-Files* he mixes a light-hearted, humorous story about three witch sisters Abbiewail, Grimly and Scarea, and their niece Hatti, with some interesting facts on animals, nature and the universe.

The witches' cousins, Flawless and Rosalind are abducted by aliens in Roswell, New Mexico and it's up to Grimly, Abbiewail, Scarea and Hatti to save them and the planet!

Well-spaced text, complimented by the author's comical illustrations, should encourage beginners to read the other two books in the **Witches** series, *The Birthday Party* and *On Vacation*.

Published by Mentor Books, 1999
ISBN 1-902586-52-2
Illustrations © Don Conroy, 1999

Published by Poolbeg Press Ltd., 2002
ISBN 1-84223-062-X

Pandora's Lunch Box by Lorraine Francis

Pandora's school lunches will never be the same again after she is given a magic lunch box by her Aunt Narcissa. But just as Mum predicts, Narcissa's brilliant schemes go a bit haywire sometimes. In fact they end up in a muddle almost all the time.

Only the Wizard Welkin can reverse the spell in exchange for Pandora's exploding orange candy crystals. Having learnt her lesson, even full roast chicken dinners with scrumptious deserts, instead of soggy ham sandwiches, aren't enough to tempt Pandora to use another of her Aunt's spells, though it might mean no homework.

Pandora's Lunch Box is a Poolbeg Goldcrest reader. Other books in this series for beginner readers by Lorraine Francis include Lulu's Tutu, Save Our Sweetshop and The Origami Bird.

Published by Macmillan Children's Books Ltd., 2001
ISBN 0-330-39731-1
Illustrations © Tony Ross, 2001

Ms Wiz – Millionaire by Terence Blacker

Terence Blacker's best-selling **Ms Wiz** stories provide the continuity of characters and storyline that appeals to young children. In this, the fifteenth, book in the series, Ms Wiz finds out she is wrong to assume that money is the most important thing in the world.

Just as the teachers complain about their local policeman and his efforts to catch a thief at St. Barnabas School, Ms Wiz arrives on the scene in her new role as private paranormal detective.

When both she and 'Dodgy Dave' Lightly become multi-millionaires from predicting the winning Lottery numbers, she realises that without magic, all that money is worthless.

Pugnax and the Princess by Dan Kissane

Contrary to what you might believe, The King of Wisdom was not the wisest man in the world. To enhance his wisdom he must get his hands on The Book of Riddles which unfortunately is the property of the ugly and deceitful Prince Pugnax of Porzana. Pugnax will only hand over the Book of Riddles in exchange for the King's daughter's hand in marriage.

This is where Agamemnon O'Sullivan an unremarkable but lucky fellow with a quick wit, and kind nature comes in. Agamemnon leaves his home to seek his fortune and ends up rescuing the princess.

This is an exciting story full of magic and fantasy, for children who can read confidently alone.

Previously published as *The King of Wisdom's Daughter*, *Pugnax and the Princess* combines the best in old Irish fairytale with modern writing for children. It is a **Red Flag Reader** from Irish Publishers, O'Brien Press specifically aimed at readers aged eight plus.

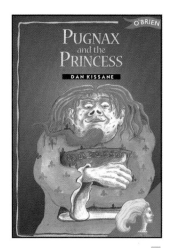

Published by The O'Brien Press Ltd., 2001
ISBN 0-86278-750-5

Published by The Penguin Group, 1978
ISBN 0-140-31108-4

The Worst Witch by Jill Murphy

This **Young Puffin** book has many of the characteristics of the earlier Puffin series such as simple sentences and pictures throughout. It continues the reading graduation from simpler books published by The Penguin Group to stories for confident readers with longer, more developed chapters.

The Worst Witch is the first in a series of stories that tell of the exploits of Mildred Hubble, the worst witch at Miss Cackle's Academy.

It's Mildred Hubble's first year at Miss Cackle's Academy for witches and she is never out of trouble. She gets her spells wrong with some very strange results. Her classmate Ethel, on the other hand, is the exact opposite – her spells always work, she's always top of the class and Miss Hardbroom is always nice to her.

Things can only get worse when Mildred turns Ethel, the teacher's pet, into a pig. In fact things get so bad that poor Mildred decides to run away, and in so doing saves the entire Academy from total disaster.

Children who have enjoyed the escapades of Harry Potter in print or on film will find many similarities and lots of equally entertaining adventures in the Worst Witch books which are more accessible to younger readers.

Read the further escapades of *The Worst Witch* in:
The Worst Witch Strikes Again
A Bad Spell for the Worst
The Worst Witch All At Sea

Sophie's Lucky   The Lion Cub   The Sheep-Pig   Care of Henry   The Enormous Crocodile

Seal of Approval   Ooh La Booga Bomp   Animals Don't Have Ghosts   Sandy the Great   The Great Pig Escape   My Dog

animals & pets

animals

& pets

Published by Walker Books Ltd., 1997
ISBN 0-7445-5258-3
Illustrations © Paul Howard, 1996

Care of Henry by Anne Fine

The **Sprinters Series** from Walker books offers more confident readers a range of humour-driven stories.

Care of Henry is one title in the series written by Anne Fine who held the position of Children's Laureate in the UK from 2001 to 2003.

The story deals in a light-hearted, humorous way with what could be a sensitive issue for Hugo, who has to decide who to stay with while mother's having a baby. A major deciding factor will be who can take the best care of his dog, Henry as well.

"Branded with the Sprinters logo, the titles in this series all have their own distinctive jackets and work equally well as stand-alone books and as part of the series."

The Children's Bookseller, 15 August 2003.

The Enormous Crocodile by Roald Dahl

This is an enchanting tale of the nasty crocodile and his many and varied plots to eat children. He is an enormous crocodile with an enormous appetite. He is the largest in the river and loves to boast to the other animals of his terrible plan. "I'm off to find a yummy child for lunch, keep listening and you'll hear the bones go crunch."

The other animals are tired of him and they make sure that his cunning plans don't go the way he wishes them to, resulting in the elephant finally whizzing him with his trunk into the hot, hot sun where he is sizzled like a sausage.

Told in typical Roald Dahl fashion, children will be fascinated by the ghastly schemes the crocodile thinks of to trap his prey.

The story is greatly enhanced by beautiful colour illustrations that in some cases provide double page backgrounds to the text.

Published by The Penguin Group, 2000
ISBN 0-14-131152-5
Illustrations © Quentin Blake, 1978

Published by Poolbeg Press Ltd., 1999
ISBN 1-85371-888-2

Seal of Approval by Don Conroy

Young Salty the sea lion's curiosity leads him into all sorts of trouble and adventures.

He unwittingly stows away on a boat, meets lots of animals and makes some good friends along the way. Even though he is young he teaches some of his new friends a thing or two about friendship and looking after others.

Four other titles, *The Bookworm Who Turned Over a New Leaf, The Anaconda from Drumcondra, The Elephant at the Door* and *Rocky the Dinosaur* complete the **Wren** series, from Poolbeg Press. Stories in this series are advertised by Poolbeg as great stories to read aloud with a child and for older readers to enjoy and collect.

Ooh La Booga Bomp by Patrice Aggs

Pintail the duck encourages all his friends to sing his newly made-up song. Refusing to take advice from Goose about the possibility of waking up the farmer, the ducks never stop to think that they could be in even greater danger. They could, and actually do, wake up The Fox.

The adventures of the farm animals are told in chronological order in a style ideally suited to beginner readers. Every page has a picture. Some entire pages are devoted to illustration. The text is well laid-out and interspersed with words in bold print, all of which will serve to attract and keep the interest of the young reader.

Ooh La Booga Bomp is Number 20 in the **O'Brien Pandas** for Beginner Readers series.

Published by The O'Brien Press Ltd., 2001
ISBN 0-86278-738-6
Illustrations © Patrice Aggs

Animals Don't Have Ghosts by Siobhán Parkinson

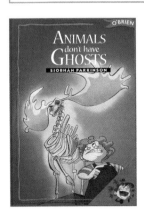

Published by The O'Brien Press Ltd., 2002
ISBN 0-86278-756-4

A **Red Flag Reader** from O'Brien Press, *Animals Don't Have Ghosts* is just right for children aged seven or eight who are ready to read what could be called a short novel. Award-winning Irish author Siobhán Parkinson strikes just the right note to appeal to children of this age.

Readers will enjoy the constant war of words between Michelle, the Dub and her country cousins, Dara and Sinead who visit the Capital for a summer holiday. They will also enjoy the never-ending series of near disasters that befall Dara, recounted with slight disdain, to say the least, by the superior Michelle.

For a complete reversal of roles why not read *Cows are Vegetarians* by the same author, describing the suddenly not-so-superior Michelle's adventures on the farm.

The Great Pig Escape by Linda Moller

Runtling, the runt of the litter, was given to a neighbouring farm because he was too small to survive on Taggerty's farm. He is a very clever pig and escapes back to Taggerty's to be with his brothers and sisters.

However, when he learns from the cat that pigs are food and are reared to be sold and eaten, he knows that he and his family will have to escape. The thirteen pigs make their escape and this book follows their adventures on the long journey.

How will the farm pigs survive in the wild and will farmer Taggerty catch up with them? This is an enjoyable animal adventure story, suitable for the more confident reader. It is one of the titles in the **Red Flag** series published by O'Brien Press.

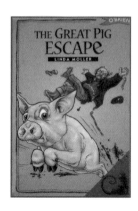

Published by The O'Brien Press Ltd., 2000
ISBN 0-862-78667-3

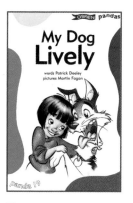

Published by The O'Brien Press Ltd., 2001
ISBN 0-86278-723-8

My Dog Lively by Patrick Deeley

Jenny wakes up on the morning of her sixth birthday, to find to her delight that she's been given a present of a collie dog. For five years she's had presents of soft toy dogs and can hardly believe it when a real live dog jumps up and bumps her on the nose.

And indeed real and live he is! Jenny decides to call him Lively and he very much lives up to his name. He barks at cats, snaps at bees, dives in the pond after the ducks and chases squirrels up trees. Just when Jenny's mum is prepared to give him a second chance, deciding he's a young dog and requires lots of patience, he gets even worse. Both Jenny and her mum decide he must go to the school for dogs.

My Dog Lively is an O'Brien **Panda** book for beginner readers and shares all the usual characteristics of books in this series; a simple but exciting storyline, lots of illustration, some words in bold print and the added bonus of a hidden panda to be found somewhere in the story.

Published by The Penguin Group, 2001
ISBN 0-141-31128-2
Illustrations © Quentin Blake, 1996

Fantastic Mr Fox by Roald Dahl

Roald Dahl's books are suitable for children of all ages and indeed also for adults who enjoy an entertaining read. *Fantastic Mr Fox* could be just the book to start young readers on a lifetime devotion to this famous writer.

Farmers Boggis, Bunce and Bean are very mean. They hate Mr Fox, and hate him even more when he gets away with their chickens, geese or turkeys. The three of them plot to kill Mr Fox and his family but they underestimate his courage and tenacity.

Children will be happy to see that Boggis, Bunce and Bean are outwitted in the end by Fantastic Mr Fox. This edition of one of Roald Dahl's most well known stories is included in the **Young Puffin** series by The Penguin Group. The series is aimed at children who have developed reading fluency.

General Field Mouse by Cora Harrison

Dragonfly Readers are a newly-published range of stories specifically aimed at young children aged between 5 and 7 years old. Carefully chosen language and vocabulary, accompanied by exciting illustrations, combine to make easy reads to be enjoyed by young children.

General Field Mouse is the bravest of all the field mice and so he is their leader. On a day when the cats come, no one will offer to help save the field mice but, like a true leader, General Field Mouse puts a clever plan into action.

Just two or three lines of text on pages containing striking illustrations are common characteristics of this and the other readers in the **Dragonfly** series by Cora Harrison. Other titles include *The Fed-Up Vacuum Cleaner, I Want a Dog* and *The Wizard of the Woods.*

Published by Mentor Press, 2002
ISBN 1-84210-147-1

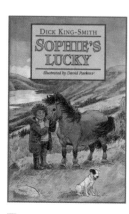

Published by Walker Books Ltd., 1995
ISBN 0-7445-4118-2
Illustrations © 1995 David Parkins

Sophie's Lucky by Dick King-Smith

This is the sixth in the series of books about Sophie, the little girl who wants to be a lady farmer when she grows up. Sophie loves animals and is the proud owner of herds of insects. She also has a snail, a rabbit, a cat, a dog and a Vietnamese pot-bellied pig.

When Sophie's elderly Aunt Al dies leaving her farm in Scotland to Sophie, it's just the beginning of the child's good fortune. On her eight birthday on Christmas Day, Sophie gets the best present imaginable; her parents present her with Lucky the pony, bought from a neighbouring farmer.

Sophie's Lucky is a story that animal lovers will get great pleasure from. Full-page illustrations with captions from the text add to this heart warming story of family life from the perspective of a discerning and amusing eight year old girl.

The Lion Cub by Eilís Dillon

Mark and his family take a day off from the farm work and go to visit the zoo. Mark takes a particular interest in the lions and coincidentally learns from the old lion keeper that his namesake, St Mark, is traditionally represented by a lion. Before they leave the zoo Mark unbelievably hides one of the cubs in the family's picnic bag and takes it home.

Looking after a lion cub on the family farm, feeding it and trying to keep it a secret, causes Mark and his sister Catherine quite a few problems. Mark realises that looking after a pet - especially a lion - is not quite as easy as he first thinks.

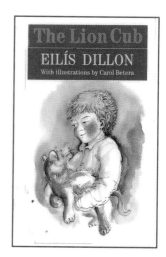

Published by Poolbeg Press Ltd., 1992
ISBN 1-85371-215-9

The Sheep-Pig by Dick King-Smith

Published by The Penguin Group, 1999
ISBN 0-141-30253-4
Illustrations © Mike Terry, 1999

This is the wonderful story of Babe, made universally famous since its release as an entertaining family film in 1995.

When Farmer Hoggett wins a pig at the fair his wife wastes no time in deciding its future. Babe is destined for the freezer but Mrs. Hoggett is completely unaware of how unusual a pig he is.

Fly, the sheep dog on the farm, fosters Babe straight away and with her constant care and tuition changes what everyone thought was an ordinary pig into a most extra ordinary "sheep-pig."

With an emphasis on politeness and manners Babe wins over the unruly sheep to do just what he wants, using the most unconventional methods. The story is packed with exciting adventures including Babe's saving the sheep from rustlers and wolves, and culminating in the little pig's triumph at the sheep dog trials.

The Sheep-Pig is a challenging read for beginners but the story is such an endearing one that once began it will just have to be finished.

Sandy the Great by Lucinda Jacob

Sandy the Great tells the story of how and when Sandy the hamster was selected at the pet shop, how he got his name and Katie's panic when he goes missing; all anecdotes to highlight that keeping a pet brings responsibility.

The author's choice of language will appeal to young readers showing an understanding of how they think and speak.

For example, "My mum is weird. First she sends me to my room to do my homework and then she comes in for a chat. I mean loopy!"

Simple pencil drawings accompany the text on every page and the lists and drawings done by Katie and her friend give examples of authentic work of children. These features will help hold the attention of reluctant readers and add to the reality of the story.

For the further adventures of Sandy read *Sandy on Holiday* by the same author.

Published by Poolbeg Press Ltd., 1999
ISBN 1-85371-916-1
Illustrations © Lucinda Jacob, 1999

The Lost Fairy   Jimmy and the Banshee   The Leprechaun Who Wished He Wasn't

fairy tales
& legends

Leprechaun On The Loose   The King's Secret   The O'Brien Book Of Irish Fairy Tales and Legends   The Names Upon The

fairy tales
& legends

Published by The O'Brien Press Ltd., 2001
ISBN 0-86278-725-4

The Lost Fairy by Marian Broderick

Flora the fairy was extremely pretty and extremely proud. She enjoyed nothing better than having the inferior snowmen and reindeer further down the Christmas tree look up to her for the whole of the holidays. She was however, a little wary of the bright star resting just below her. Incredible as it seemed, she had heard of some people who put a star at the top of the Christmas tree instead of a fairy.

Flora had sat on her first tree ninety years ago and wasn't going to give up her place to any silly star. Then on Christmas Eve, Flora falls off the tree and the family are too busy to put her back up. Fortunately Lily the Little comes to the rescue and Flora finds you're never too old or too pretty to learn a lesson.

The Lost Fairy is a **Yellow Flag Reader** and is one of the stories in the **Flyers** series by O'Brien Press, best suited to children aged between six and eight years old.

Jimmy and the Banshee by Dan Kissane

Jimmy McElhatton is surprised when he meets an unusual woman down at the Hegarty's old place. Strangers don't appear very often in his village. Jimmy has a funny feeling that he needs to put some distance between himself and this lady. Then he meets another, standing on the footbridge at night! Who are they? What do they want?

A strange symbol carved on a flat, black rock by the well at the back of Hegarty's house also has a particular significance.

Children will enjoy Dan Kissane's humorous descriptions. For example, Jimmy describes his friend as having "one of those faces that looks as though someone has sat on it, and with his red hair standing up in spikes, he looked like he had been dragged backwards through a hedge."

Published by The O'Brien Press Ltd., 1999
ISBN 0-86278-549-9

This story will acquaint today's schoolchildren with one of the common myths of old Ireland, the banshee. The banshee of Irish mythology is portrayed in a hair-raising adventure story that's sure to grab the attention of young readers.

The Lost Fairy Jimmy and the Banshee The Leprechaun Who Wished He Wasn't Leprechaun On The Loose The King's

The Leprechaun Who Wished He Wasn't by Siobhan Parkinson

Published by The O'Brien Press Ltd., 1993
ISBN 0-86278-334-8

Complete with a glossary explaining words like *amadán*, *eejit* and *ogham*, this book, suited to children aged 6 plus, contains an exciting mix of old Irish words and up-to-the-minute expressions. When his fellow leprechauns disapprove of Laurence's attempts to reform his character, and ask what's wrong with being a leprechaun, Laurence replies "It's too corny, it's just not cool. All the really hip people are human beings."

When he gets discovered by Phoebe he insists he's a "huming" being just like her.

The conversation between the two carries the reader along. Laurence's transformation from leprechaun to gremlin produces some entertaining incidents.

An entertaining and challenging read first published in 1993, and now as a **Yellow Flag Reader** by O'Brien Press.

Leprechaun On The Loose by Annette Kelleher

Biddy the leprechaun is sick and tired of looking after her father's gold and of the constant rain. When Corey, on holiday from Australia overhears her, saying she'd trade her gold for a week of sunshine, he makes her an offer she can't refuse.

Biddy swaps her gold for his passport and takes off for a week to Australia. When she gets back home, her troubles start! Biddy has lost Corey's passport and Corey won't part with the gold.

A **Red Flag Reader** by O'Brien Press, *Leprechaun on the Loose* is suited to children aged 8 and up with a generous helping of humour to engage young readers.

Published by The O'Brien Press Ltd., 2001
ISBN 0-86278-729-7

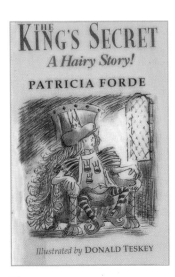

Published by The O'Brien Press Ltd., 1993
ISBN 0-86278-340-2

The King's Secret by Patricia Forde

The King's Secret is a modern retelling of the old story of King Lowry Lynch and his horses' ears in a unique new style that will appeal to young children.

Lowry's mother, Queenie is quite proud of her son whom she thinks is a very good king. He has always gone to bed without a word, never given back-answers and is quite good about tidying his room; just the kind of behaviour you would expect from a king!!! But even perfect kings will pose problems for their mums at some stage or another. Lowry simply will not have his hair cut. No way! And to add insult to injury, he always wears an ugly, battered old hat on top of his curly locks that block the sink and fall in his soup.

Read how Lowry and Seamus, his young barber, bring their pretentious mothers down to earth with a jolt in this amusing retelling of one of Ireland's famous legends.

The O'Brien Book of Irish Fairy Tales and Legends Retold by Una Leavy

This is a beautiful collection of some of the most famous Irish legends; stories of fairies and giants, stories of good and evil, and of love and hatred. Una Leavy brings to life these mysterious and magical tales of long ago for young readers.

With powerful Celtic illustrations by Susan Field and ancient stories that keep Ireland's past alive, the book will be cherished by old and young alike.

There is a short background to each story outlining its place in history, at the back of the book. Stories like *How Cúchulainn Got His Name*, *Tír na n-Óg* and *The Children of Lir* are written in an easy style for children to read themselves and are equally suitable stories to share.

Published by The O'Brien Press Ltd., 1996
ISBN 0-86278-482-4
Illustrations © Susan Field, 1996

The Names Upon The Harp by Marie Heaney

The Names Upon The Harp is a collection of classic Irish legends divided into the three main cycles of Irish literature as explained by the author. A brief introduction to each cycle provides the background to well known stories of Old Ireland such as Finn and the Salmon of Knowledge or Oisín in the Land of Youth, and some not so well known tales including Bricriu's Feast and The Enchanted Deer. A useful pronunciation guide is provided giving separate pronunciation notes for each story with an extensive bibliography at the end.

Like *The O'Brien Book of Irish Fairy Tales and Legends*, this collection could be just as enjoyable for children to listen to as to read. Striking illustrations by award-winning illustrator P.J. Lynch make this a book to treasure for the whole family.

Published by Faber and Faber Ltd., 2000
ISBN 0-571-19363-3
Illustrations © P.J. Lynch, 2000

tales
with
a
twists

tales
with a
twist

Published by Wolfhound Press, 1998
ISBN 0-86327-669-5
Illustrations © Marie-Louise Fitzpatrick, 1998

Fionn the Cool by Aislinn O'Loughlin

Fionn the Cool is an amusing and clever send-up of the ancient Irish story of Fionn Mac Cumhaill. Other books by Aislinn O'Loughlin written in the same vein include *Cinderella's Fella, Shak and the Beanstalk, A Right Royal Pain* and *The Emperor's Birthday Suit.*

The settings of the first two chapters of *Fionn the Cool* couldn't be more different. The reader is transported from Celtic times to O'Connell Street, Dublin in 1998, and so too are two teenage boys coincidentally named Fionn and Diarmuid. They progress from referring to cars as "big, metal, chariotty thingys," to wearing jeans and T-shirts in an effort to act like Irish teenagers of the 20th century.

This is an excellent time-travel story with lots of humour that will appeal to readers of eight and up, from an author whose books have been described as "….bright, sharp and full of fun" by the *Irish Times* and "devilishly clever stuff" by the *RTE Guide.*

Wolfgran by Finbar O' Connor

This is a comic sequel to the fairy tale *Little Red Riding Hood*. After her narrow escape from the wolf, Granny decides the forest is too dangerous for her and sells her cottage. She moves into the Happy-ever-after-Home for Retired Fairy-tale Characters.
The wolf misses Granny and, disguising himself as an old lady, he follows her, swallowing everyone he happens to come in contact with. With the aid of the bungling Inspector Plonker and his second-in-command, Sergeant Snoop, Little Red Riding Hood saves the day. As with all fairy-tales, everyone, (except the wolf) lives happily ever after.
Wolfgran is a **Red Flag Reader** from O'Brien Press.

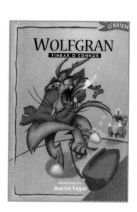

Published by The O'Brien Press Ltd., 2001
ISBN 0-86278-730-0

Molly and the Beanstalk by Pippa Goodhart

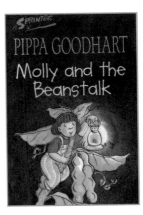

Books by popular children's authors like Philippa Pearce, Dick King-Smith, Anne Fine and Colin McNaughton make up the **Sprinters** series published by Walker Books. They are ideal first books for beginner readers. Well-spaced text in large print with plenty of illustration will entice children as young as five or six to read them.

Little Molly sows a story seed just by wishing she could see new places and meet new people. As the clouds melt away and the weather gets hotter the story begins. Many problems have to be solved before Molly can have her happy ever after ending. She and Old Ma are saved from starvation by a giant Molly who provides the ending Little Molly needs. A *Jack-in-the Beanstalk* story with a difference!

Published by Walker Books Ltd., 2001
ISBN 0-7445-5981-2
Illustrations © Brita Granström, 2001

Cinderella's Fella by Aislinn O'Loughlin

Cinderella's Fella is a witty rendition of the story of Cinderella told from Prince Fred Charming's viewpoint. Fred's father has arranged a huge ball to celebrate his son's eighteenth birthday - but there's a catch. Prince Fred must choose a wife at the ball.

The preparations get under way immediately with Fred's stepmom Queen Sandra donning her apron and returning to the kitchen to help out. After all Sandra was a kitchen girl by birth! Fred advises his young twin sisters not to believe in those stupid bedtime fairy stories where beautiful girls appear out of the blue, win the prince's heart and live happily ever after, which is in fact just what he ends up doing himself.

Published by Wolfhound Press, 1995
ISBN 0-86327-493-5
Illustrations © Marie-Louise Fitzpatrick

The Karate Princess by Jeremy Strong

Princess Belinda was the youngest of sixteen girls. Her fifteen sisters were beautiful princesses, but not Belinda. Ignored by her father, Belinda's mother, the queen, decided she needed a tutor. Hiro Ono teaches the princess how to survive and win a husband with her brain – not her looks.

When given the opportunity to marry the local prince she has to prove herself braver than her rival, Princess Samandra, but this is no problem for Belinda, the karate expert.

Six chapters combine to tell the tale of a very uncharacteristic princess. Humour is a common trait in all Jeremy Strong's books and *The Karate Princess* is certainly full of fun.

Published by The Penguin Group, 1989
ISBN 0-14-032804-1
Illustrations © Simone Abel, 1986

**social
issues**

*social
issues*

Stranger Danger? by Anne Fine

Stranger Danger? is the perfect book to facilitate discussion with young children about talking to strangers.

Following a talk given by a policeman in school, Joe has a number of tough decisions to make. Does he simply follow the Eye Test Lady whom he has never seen before, even though he's just been told never go with a stranger? Does he take a peppermint in the concert hall from a kind old gentleman to help him stop coughing, even though he's been advised never take sweets from a stranger?

There are five short chapters in this **Young Puffin** book which is ideally suited for confidence building in solo reading.

Published by The Penguin Group, 1991
ISBN 0-14-034302-4-
Illustrations © Jean Bayliss, 1989

Walter Speazlebud by David Donohue

This is the story of Walter and his unusual family. His father is an inventor, his mum an artist and his granddad a very talented wood carver who, like Walter, possesses the gift of "noitanigami" or imagination spelt backwards.

The power of "noitanigami" can make people go backwards in time but it can only be used to help others. When Mr Strong, Walter's horrible teacher, starts picking on him, he had better watch out. So too had class bully, Danny Biggles.

Walter Speazlebud touches on topics such as learning difficulties, bullying, old age and dying from a child's perspective. In this **Red Flag Reader** from O'Brien Press, David Donohue has successfully stepped into the mind and "noitanigami" of a 9 year old boy.

Published by The O'Brien Press Ltd., 2002
ISBN 0-86278-762-9

Adam's Starling by Gillian Perdue

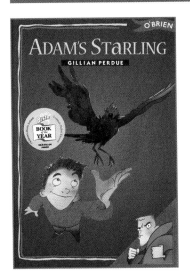

Published by The O'Brien Press Ltd., 2001
ISBN 0-86278-685-1

Adam's Starling won the Bisto Book of the Year/Eilis Dillon Award in 2002 for the author's first outstanding children's book.

Life is difficult all round for Adam; he is bullied at school and at home he feels no-one has any time for him. His mum is concerned about the possibility of losing her job, his Dad works nights and Adam's grandfather, who constantly mistakes Adam for his son, is in a nursing home.

At school it's worse. Adam is bullied by three boys in his class

But Adam finds a secret, special friend in a scruffy, brown starling that he feeds regularly every day. When the school bullies bring Adam's starling into class to frighten him, it is the last straw for Adam. It is also a defining moment in his life.

Somehow he finds the courage he never thought he had to defend this little bird, and in so doing he confronts his enemies. Adam's Starling is a **Red Flag Reader** from O'Brien Press and like all titles in the series it is ideally suited to children aged 8 and over. It is an encouraging story for any young reader who has experienced the typical worries of childhood with the added trauma of being bullied at school.

Published by The Penguin Group, 1995
ISBN 0-14-036429-3
Illustrations © Barry Wilkinson, 1994

Jimmy Woods and the Big Bad Wolf by Mick Gowar

Jimmy Woods is a compulsive bully who hurts people because he likes to. After he terrorizes all the kids on the road and robs their pocket money, he sets his sights on bigger things. He manages to secure a key of old Granny Simpson's back door and regularly threatens her, eats her food and tries to get hold of her pension book.

But there is one thing Jimmy is really scared of....dogs, especially Prince the hero of the story. This is an exciting story for young children, with underlying morals subtly introduced. The theme of bullying is very strong, and so also is the subject of caring for the elderly.

Jimmy Woods and the Big Bad Wolf is a story from the **Chillers** series by Puffin which features thrillers, ghost stories and mysteries for children. Excellent storylines are presented in a variety of text styles, often appearing on an illustrated background.

Ms Cliff the Climber by Allan Ahlberg

The **Happy Families** books by Allan Ahlberg are guaranteed to deal with everyday issues in the funniest, madcap stories you've ever read. In *Ms Cliff the Climber* Clara Cliff spends all her time climbing through the ups and downs of life.

She meets and marries Clifford Clamber and they have a baby girl called Clarissa. However, as time goes by Clara and Clifford divorce. Clara and Clarissa live together for some time and then Clara meets and marries Claude who has three children of his own.

Through its portrayal of totally chaotic family life, the story deals in a unique and humourous way with marriage, divorce and mixed siblings. On the surface it's just a funny story but could be a great launch pad for discussion about everyday issues for today's children.

Full colour illustrations with a substantial amount of text make **Happy Families** ideal beginner readers for young children.

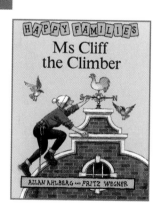

Published by The Penguin Group, 1997
ISBN 0-670-86591-5
Illustrations © Fritz Wegner, 1997

The Angel of Nitshill Road by Anne Fine

Any book from multiple award-winning author, Anne Fine is guaranteed to be a runaway success. *The Angel of Nitshill Road* is no different. A book for younger readers, it tells the story of how life changed at Nitshill Road School for Penny, Mark and Marigold once the angel arrived.

The author describes with striking accuracy Penny's fear of being bullied and teased in the playground because of her weight, by the school bully, Barry Hunter. Mark, the nervous child, can't contain his rage when Barry teases him and ends up going completely crazy, which is exactly what Barry wants. Marigold simply endures all the taunts, her expression never changing.

Even when writing about such a serious matter, Anne Fine provides the usual helping of humour, characteristic of all her books. Mr. Fairway is completely at a loss when it comes to dealing with Celeste, (the angel of the story) in class. Her suggestions are always unusual but he ends up letting her have her way time after time.

Before she leaves the school, not only has she solved the bullying problem, but Celeste has made Mr. Fairway promise it will never happen again as long as he is teaching in Nitshill Road School.

Published by Mammoth, 1993
ISBN 0-7497-0974-X
Illustrations © Kate Aldous, 1992

Bullies at School by Theresa Breslin

Siobhan Cunningham dreads walking past the usual gang of bullies who wait at the school gates for her every morning, some of whom used to be her friends. Things go from bad to worse, up to a point where the teachers, knowing nothing of her problems, send for Siobhan's mother. Only the kind librarian, Mrs Allen has an inclination of what's going on.

When she takes Siobhan on a visit to the Resource Centre, it becomes the turning point in her life. The Celtic brooch she finds there gives her the power to stand up to her mean friends, but unfortunately begins to turn her into someone like them. She has to be careful to use her new power, not to abuse it.

Bullies at School is an exciting fast-paced story suitable for children who are comfortable with independent reading.

Published by Blackie Children's Books, 1993
ISBN 0-216-94038-9
Illustrations © Lynne Willey, 1993

for Plover Hill Katie's Cake Bert's Wonderful News Ramona and her Mother

Impossible Parents Chalk and Cheese Just-the-Same Jamie Jigsaw Stew Danny and Baby Do It All The Fight

The Mum-Minder   Impossible Parents   Chalk and Cheese   Just-the-Same Jamie

families

D.C

Jigsaw Stew   Danny and Baby Do It All   The Fight for Plover Hill   Katie's Cake   Bert's Wonderful News

families

Impossible Parents by Brian Patten

Impossible Parents, a **Sprinters** book from Walker is ideally suited to the child who has decided he wants to read by himself. Five short chapters containing pages with lots of quirky drawings and comic strips are just what beginner readers need to encourage them to read more and to develop confidence in independent reading.

Ben and Mary's Dad sports a stupid filthy ponytail, dangling from the back of his head and wears a daft earring in the corner of his right nostril. Their mum who is a belly dancer dresses in fishnet body stockings.

Published by Walker Books Ltd., 1995
ISBN 0-7445-3668-5
Illustrations © Arthur Robins, 1994

That's not so bad until teacher announces she's looking forward to meeting all parents on Parents' Day on Friday. Children will enjoy the sibling camaraderie displayed in the schemes hatched by Ben and Mary to ensure their parents don't embarrass them.

Chalk and Cheese by Adèle Geras

Jo and Lily are sisters. Jo loves ballet, frills and pink clothes. Lily thinks they are soppy and loves to play pirates and wants to learn judo. However both girls find something they can enjoy in the Christmas ballet, The Nutcracker.

The story outlines the differences between sisters in most families. Jo, the girlie girl and Lily the tomboy can see those differences in one another and can easily accept them. They manage to change most circumstances to suit their very different personalities.

Chalk and Cheese is a story from the **Corgi Pups** series which is perfect for beginner readers.

Published by Corgi Pups, 1996
ISBN 0-552-52971-0
Illustrations © Adriano Gon, 1996

Published by Poolbeg Press Ltd., 2000
ISBN 1-84223-003-4

Just-the-Same Jamie by Malachy Doyle

Just as the title says Jamie likes everything to be just the same. Every morning he eats his cornflakes from his red and white stripy bowl, wears the same clothes and descends the stairs two at a time.

When a totally transformed Aunt Alice visits he's not at all pleased with her appearance until he sees her new, super-charged motorbike. She's wearing a shiny black leather suit and, even better, she's got one for Jamie too. Jamie discovers it's cool to dress differently and do different things but it's good to return to routine also.

Large bold print and lots of simple drawings, characteristic of **Poolbeg Goldcrest** readers, will appeal to young children.

Jigsaw Stew by Conor McHale

Times are hard for the MacAnoolie family. The severe snows have left them without food. The resourceful Mrs MacAnoolie can make a meal out of all kinds of everything – furniture, bicycles, books, to name just a few of her favourite ingredients.

But when she makes a jigsaw stew to feed the family she discovers that being resourceful isn't always good. Using his trousers, a branch from a tree, and a strong gust of wind, Jack and Doctor Mulgrew save the day.

Jigsaw Stew is one of the **O'Brien Flyers** series for children who can read confidently alone. Some elements of the totally farcical story will remind children of their own families, particularly brothers whose sisters drive them crazy! Hilarious pictures complement an equally funny text, with an added surprise for young readers on the last page.

Published by The O'Brien Press Ltd., 2000
ISBN 0-86278-688-6
Illustrations © Conor McHale, 2000

The Fight Danny and Baby Do It All Just-the-Same Jamie Jigsaw Stew Chalk and Cheese Impossible Parents

Danny and Baby Do It All by Brianóg Brady Dawson

Poor old Danny Brown is suffering from a bad case of sibling jealousy. Everyone knows that reaching the age of one is no big deal but Susie continues to get loads and loads of presents for her first birthday. The Baby Do It All dolly from Gran was the worst; she looked silly, her legs were bent and fat and she had no hair.

For everyone else, Baby Do It All is fantastic. She laughs, she cries and best of all she wets! For Danny this is the worst thing about the doll. Matters go from bad to worse when Danny decides to make the doll pay for destroying his gun caps.

Other stories about Danny include, *Danny's Smelly Toothbrush* and *Danny's Sick Trick* all available in the **Panda** series from O'Brien Press.

Published by The O'Brien Press Ltd., 2000
ISBN 0-86278-690-8

The Fight for Plover Hill by Eilís Dillon

A family adventure story, *The Flight for Plover Hill* is a **Red Flag Reader** from O'Brien Press and is suitable children's fiction for children aged 8 and over.

Old Dan Flaherty refuses to leave his farm on Plover Hill even when it is surrounded by water and it becomes an island. He has lived there all his life – as had his father and his grandfather. With the help of his grandson John, he is determined to save the farm and its four-legged inhabitants from greedy property developers.

Published by The O'Brien Press Ltd., 2001
ISBN 0-86278-709-2

Katie's Cake by Stephanie Dagg

With only one or two sentences on every page, humourous drawings and an added challenge to spot the panda hidden in the story, O'Brien **Panda** books will attract and sustain the interest of young children.

The rainbow cake baked by Mum for Auntie Susan's visit is just too much for Katie to resist despite Mum's warnings. When she's tried all the different coloured icing and then tried them all over again to see which one tastes best, she realises she's down to the cake. What does Katie do next? Read about her unbelievable efforts to restore the icing on the cake.

This is the second "Katie" book by Stephanie Dagg, in the **O'Brien Pandas** series which is perfect for first readers who are beginning to make their own way through books.

Published by The O'Brien Press Ltd., 1999
ISBN 0-86278-617-7

Published by Walker Books Ltd., 1998
ISBN 0-7445-5914-6
Illustrations © Brita Granström, 1998

Bert's Wonderful News by Sam McBratney

Bert's Wonderful News is a perfect selection of stories for young readers to enjoy alone. Seven independent chapters can be read individually as self-contained stories that young children will identify with. All together they provide an interesting account of Bert's life with his dad and his dad's friend Liz whom Bert likes very much.

Bert feels he never has any News to tell at school, so when he gets lost in a big department store with moving stairs and nice smells, he is sure it's never happened to Charlie or Meg or Geraldine Greer and it will be his big news for teacher.

But as always Geraldine Greer spoils his news by telling the whole story to teacher and all his classmates before he gets a chance to speak.

But Bert's most wonderful news of all comes when Dad tells him he is going to marry Liz and this time even Geraldine Greer can't spoil the story.

Ramona and her Mother by Beverly Cleary

A warning on the front cover sums up what the story is about, "mothers shouldn't think being seven and a half is easy – because it isn't!"

Above all else, Ramona would like her mother's attention just to herself for a while but it seems this is an impossible request. Mrs Quimby is a busy working mother and sometimes doesn't even notice how hard Ramona tries to be loved. She would love to be called "her mother's girl" or to hear her Mum say she couldn't manage without her.

Because Ramona's mother and father both go out to work Willa Jean's granny looks after her every day after school. Ramona's concerns and worries are relayed in an amazingly true-to-life way by the author and will strike a chord with working mothers everywhere.

A phone call from Ramona's teacher is just what the whole family needs to have an open discussion about all their woes and to realise that their problems can be overcome.

Beverly Cleary is one of America's most popular authors and has won many prestigious awards, including the American Library Association's Laura Ingalls Wilder Award.

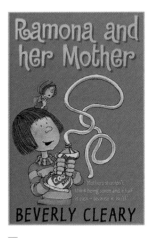

Published by Oxford University Press, 2001
ISBN 0-19-275104-2

Published by Corgi Yearling, 1994
ISBN 0-440-86302-3
Illustrations © Nick Sharratt, 1993

The Mum-Minder by Jacqueline Wilson

Jacqueline Wilson is renowned for her sensitive treatment of ordinary issues common to today's children. *The Mum-Minder* deals in the author's inimitable and humourous way with Sadie's mum's dilemma when she falls ill.

When Mum gets the flu, Sadie not only takes her place as child minder to the babies she cares for; she also becomes a mum-minder. It's her half-term but instead of having a break from school she spends her time looking after three-year-old Gemma, two-year-old Vincent, baby Clive and her own baby sister, Sara.

But loyal to their motto, "us girls have got to stick together", Sadie, with the help of all the mums, copes until her mum is back on her feet again.

The Mum-Minder is a **Corgi Yearling** book ideally suited to children who have mastered the art of reading alone. The typically funny illustrations by Nick Sharratt add to the appeal of the story for young readers.

adventure
stories

adventure
stories

Published by Poolbeg Press Ltd., 2000
ISBN 1-85371-928-5

Save our Sweetshop by Lorraine Francis

Benny, Rita, Frankie and Denis are friends. Every weekend when they get their pocket money they go to The Nook – a real sweetshop owned by two sisters Dolly and Nancy.

The adventure begins when the council announce their plans to demolish the shop because it is unsafe.

The Nook is not just any old sweetshop. It's full of the most wonderful treats supplied with special recommendations from Dolly, the nicer of the two sisters, who is always chewing and loves sweets as much as the children themselves do.

Under no circumstances can the four friends allow the sweetshop to be knocked down. Through various schemes they pull out all the stops to renovate the shop and keep it open, jumble sales, protest marches and miracles included!

Save Our Sweetshop is an easy read for children aged between 6 and 9. It is just one title in the **Poolbeg Wren** series which is ideally aimed at children who are beginning to read on their own.

Reggie the Stuntman by Kate Shannon

Reggie the Stuntman from the **Collins Colour Jets** series is a great story to engage the imagination. All stories in this series are full of action, adventure, crazy incidents and unusual characters.

Reggie and his stunt cat Tallulah may not be famous but they get their pictures taken with all the stars. When Rathbone D. Hammond phones from his office in L.A. it's all systems go again for these two movie heroes. Previous films Reggie has worked on provide the clues to the mystery of the missing director and the solution to finding him.

Colour Jets offer an excellent variety of text presentation to sustain the young reader's interest from page to page. Comic-style speech bubbles mixed together with traditional lines of writing, and striking illustrations which sometimes provide the background for the entire page, make this series one of the best for beginner readers.

Published by HarperCollins Ltd., 1998
ISBN 0-00-675357-4
Illustrations © Kate Shannon, 1998

Carrot Thompson Record Breaker by Malachy Doyle

From the day she was born Carrot Thompson was a record breaker. For her eighth birthday she gets a stopwatch from her parents and The Biggest Book of Records from Gran. That's when trouble begins.

Now Carrot has no end of possible tasks she can try in an effort to break world records. She even sets a new record getting ready for bed in 2 minutes and 26.928 seconds.

When Carrot and her friend Marcus eventually decide on creating The One Leg Clapping Record parents and teachers had better beware.

A **Poolbeg Wren** book, *Carrot Thompson Record Breaker* has just the right mix of humour, well-spaced, easy-to-read text and comical illustrations by Leonard O'Grady to entice young readers.

Published by Poolbeg Press Ltd., 2000
ISBN 1-85371-932-3

Zesty by Sam McBratney

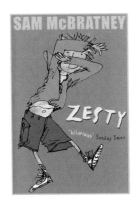

Macmillan Children's Books Ltd., 2002
ISBN 0-330-39987-X
Illustration © Tim Archbold, 2002

Sam Mc Bratney has written extensively for children of all ages. His picture book *Guess How Much I Love You* is one of the most successful books in the history of children's literature. The blundering Jimmy Zest is the hero of several of his books.

In *Zesty* Jimmy has loads of "good" ideas to act upon with his old friends Shorty, Legweak, Mandy Taylor, Gowso, Knuckles and Penny Brown. It is with these five mates that Jimmy Zest shares his plans and hair-brained ideas in five separate stories.

The ingenuity of Jimmy will appeal to readers in the first story Giant Money-boxes when he sells fillings for April crackers from a collection of goodies he has stored in his desk drawer at school. This is yet another scheme for Jimmy's mission in life: that is to make money.

The remaining four chapters are just as action-packed, full of foul play, comedy and adventure to make this second collection of stories every bit as good as *Jimmy Zest*, the first book in the series.

Knut and Freya in Wales by Mary Arrigan

Knut and Freya in Wales is a **Poolbeg Wren** story book. It is as suitable for reading aloud to a child as it is for the young reader to attempt alone.

Knut's mum, Helga the Huge allows four Welsh strangers to steal Freya's Da, Sven the Blacksmith. Helga the Huge blames her son Knut who, instead of advising her to be polite, should have been "thumping those people about" like they normally would have done with people who wandered in."

The story has all the ingredients of a rescue adventure. Knut the hero sets out to rescue his tearful friend's Da who is being held hostage by Queen Awllbrann in her Welsh castle. But in doing so he saves the entire kingdom from the invading Saxons, through a combination of wooden helmets, lots of wood shavings and lots of singing.

Published by Poolbeg Press Ltd., 2000
ISBN 1-85371-914-5

Published by Mentor Press, 1998
ISBN 1-902586-02-6

Escape the Volcano by Stephanie Dagg

A holiday in France turns into an exciting adventure for Tom, when he. and his family stay in a gîte overlooking one of France's dormant volcanoes. Tom has inherited his fascination with volcanoes from his Dad who died two years earlier.

For the first time in months Mum seems truly happy and Tom is determined to keep her that way. In fact the concern he has for his Mum is an underlying theme of the whole story.

Even when Tom, his friend Kevin and his sister Anna get trapped in underground caves they can't help but appreciate the adventure as they marvel at the stalagmites and find cave drawings.

The research carried out by their new friend, a scientist who is studying the same cave system, helps to lead them to safety. The story ends with Tom's realisation that he will be seeing a lot more of Alan the scientist in future, as his friendship with Mum deepens.

Other titles in this series for independent readers by Stephanie Dagg include *Escape the Avalanche, Escape the Flood* and *Escape the Twister.*

Charlie Harte and His Two-Wheeled Tiger by Frank Murphy

Charlie would love a bike more than anything but his family can't afford one. When he sees an old bike frame left for the refuse collection his plans to create his own bike from scrap begin. Searching for the parts he needs in Flanagan's scrapyard leads to a long and lasting friendship and even a business partnership with Miko, the owner.

Tiger becomes the coolest bike in the neighbourhood with its black, white and yellow stripes, and even though it comes last in the school sports bike race, it has hidden powers and takes on a whole life of its own. Charlie's bike may not be "cool" but it sure is different. Charlie's bike can talk!!

Published by The O'Brien Press Ltd., 1997
ISBN 0-86278-532-4

Charlie Harte and His Two-Wheeled Tiger is a **Red Flag Reader** from O'Brien Press. Divided into twenty chapters it will give young readers the feeling of reading a "real" book without presenting them with a difficult vocabulary. The story introduces the many interesting themes that children will identify with in a language that's both humourous and meaningful.

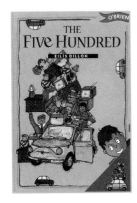

Published by The O'Brien Press Ltd., 1991
ISBN 0-86278-262-7

The Five Hundred by Eilís Dillon

Luca has saved for over a year and bought a Fiat Five Hundred. Now that he has a car he can bring more goods to market, and as a result make more money.

However, not everyone is happy with his success and disaster strikes when the Five Hundred is stolen. Pierino, Luca's son, is a clever child and his intuition prompts him to follow the rather strange policeman investigating the case, and in so doing he finds out who the thieves are.

He and Luca are reunited with their Five Hundred just in the nick of time before it gets scrapped.

The Five Hundred is a **Red Flag Reader** from O'Brien Press and is a thrilling adventure story set against the lifestyles of the Roman people and the city of Rome towards the end of the twentieth century.

Dimanche Diller by Henrietta Branford

Dimanche Diller won the Smarties Book Prize in 1994. The story is a challenging one and is probably best suited to readers aged at least 8. In the opening paragraph we are advised not to look forward to a happy ending because fate has dealt the heroine, Dimanche several cruel blows.

Dimanche's woes began after a kind fisherman and his wife decided to hand her over to the village priest, having found her little body adrift on the Mediterranean Sea.

When the evil Valburga Vilemile, posing as Dimanche's aunt, notices an old advertisement in the personal column of The Times detailing the shipwreck and the history of baby Dimanche, it's all she needs to develop a plan to get rich.

Even Polly Pugh, Dimanche's nanny and true friend cannot prevent this evil woman from trying to kill her on many occasions. "Teach the child deep-sea diving," she suggested as soon as Dimanche could swim. "Never mind the treacherous tides, you mustn't mollycoddle her," she would say in yet another effort to get her hands on Dimanche's vast inheritance.

This is a story full of adventure which will capture the imagination and sustain the reader's interest right to the end.

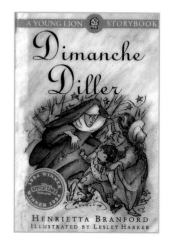

Published by Collins Children's Books, 1994
ISBN 0-00-674748-5
Illustrations © Lesley Harker, 1994

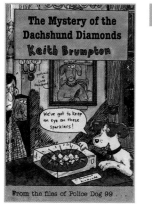

The Mystery of the Dachshund Diamonds by Keith Brumpton

For a child who likes reading comics *The Mystery of the Dachshund Diamonds* provides just the right mix of comic text and illustration along with the characteristic layout of traditional "chapter books" for young readers. Ten short chapters tell the funny story of Rusty the police dog and PC Andy Constable's quest to find the thieves who are trying to steal the Daschund diamonds.

Both are on their last chance. In an effort to solve the crime they must become undercover agents or else face re-assignment. Packed with adventure and comedy this is an ideal beginner book for any reluctant reader.

Published by Orchard Books, 1995
ISBN 1-85213-886-6

Rita the Rescuer by Hilda Offen

Rita Potter is the youngest in her family. Her older brothers and sisters don't want to play with her because, according to them, she needs to be minded all the time.

But one day Rita proves them wrong when a parcel arrives for her. In the parcel is a rescuer's outfit. Rita puts it on and is transformed into a most daring heroine helping people in the most incredibly dangerous situations. Other books about this courageous heroine include; *Roll Up! Roll Up! It's Rita*, *SOS for Rita* and *Rita in Wonderland*.

All are titles in the **First Young Puffin** series. Lively, easy-to read stories and colour illustrations on every page are characteristic of this extensive range of beginner readers for children.

Published by The Penguin Group, 1997
ISBN 0-14-038598-3

Joe's Bike Race by Malachy Doyle

When Miss Blackburn announces there's no money for the school camping trip, Joe decides to fund raise for it. With the help of his dad he organises a bike race. The most amazing bicycles turn up, like Pete's with a trailer attached, home to the sleeping twins, or the Firebrigandem carrying seven firemen.

Joe's Bike Race is a **Poolbeg Goldcrest Reader**. Books in the series are characterised by simple language in large type and lots of amusing illustrations to sustain the interest of beginner readers as young as five or six.

Published by Poolbeg Press Ltd., 2001
ISBN 1-84223-025-5

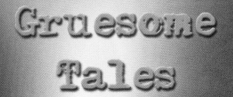

Gruesome Tales

Gruesome Tales

Published by Walker Books Ltd.,
ISBN 0-7445-2435-0
Illustrations © Arthur Robins, 1992

The Finger Eater by Dick King-Smith

The Finger Eater was first published by Walker Books in1992. It was re-launched in the **Sprinters** series in 1994 and is still a great children's favourite. Dick King-Smith is one of the world's favourite children's authors and has won numerous awards for his writing.

In this rather gruesome story which is not for the faint-hearted, Ulf the nasty finger-eating troll meets his match in the crafty little girl, Gudrun who tricks him into eating a deer antler, thinking it was her hand.

Lots of amusing comic-style illustrations separate the text, some of which is also written in comic-book style. Dick King-Smith is renowned for his witty portrayal of human and animal behaviour which is very much in evidence in this story.

Red Eyes at Night by Michael Morpurgo

Michael Morpurgo writes for children of all ages and for teenagers also. His books have won many awards, and he became Children's Laureate in 2003.

Red Eyes at Night is a funny story written in a chatty style in the first person. It is also a story with a spooky twist.

Every summer Millie's cousin the perfect Geraldine comes to stay, and it's up to Millie to entertain her. It wouldn't be too bad if Geraldine wasn't so good at everything. Gran and Mum think she's wonderful and even Bingo the dog will go to no one else when Geraldine's around.

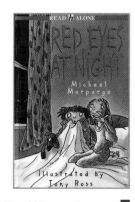

Published by Hodder Children's Books, 1998
ISBN 0-340-68753-3
Illustrations © Tony Ross, 1998

When Millie discovers that Geraldine is afraid of ghosts she devises a plan to take her down a peg or two. But the best laid plans are often doomed to backfire.

The Bodigulpa by Jenny Nimmo

Published by Macmillan Children's Books Ltd., 2001
ISBN 0-330-39750-8
Illustrations © David Roberts, 2001

The Bodigulpa comes from a spine-tingling series of **Shock Shop Stories**. A short prologue to the story gives a taste of the gruesome tale to follow.

Daniel's garden seems like the ideal haven for young boys; untended, full of big leafy plants and best of all it comes complete with an empty greenhouse which functions as Starship Danmatt 1 for Daniel and his friend Matt. That was until Grandpa Green came to stay!

He takes over Daniel's greenhouse for his horrible, trailing, whispering plants. Not only are his plants horrible but so is he. He is dirty and bad-mannered and Daniel is sure he has something to do with the disappearance of Grandma, of his Auntie Lorna, and her dog, Stanley.

When he admits to Daniel that his Bodigulpa plant is a carnivore it's clear there's something very sinister going on.

"A great story, brilliantly told and bursting with horror, laughter and black, black humour!" *Amazon*

Hairy Bill by Susan Price

Another story in the **Shock Shop** series, *Hairy Bill* is a short scary story for younger readers. The story opens with a scratching and muttering in Alex's unused bedroom fireplace and, whatever it is, it most certainly is not Father Christmas.

Alex's mum comes from the Black Isle in Scotland. The Matheson's farm had always been haunted by a bogle so when Aunt Jennie dies the bogle, Hairy Bill, comes to live with them.

When the bogle first arrives Alex is not too put out by his presence but he soon changes his mind. Not before he causes total mayhem both inside and outside the house does the family manage to get rid of Hairy Bill.

Published by Macmillan Children's Books Ltd., 2002
ISBN 0-333-96256-7
Illustrations © Chris Riddell, 2002

Seven short chapters tell the story of this unusual monster and his exploits, complemented by excellent drawings by Chris Riddell. Like all books in the series Hairy Bill is suited to young readers who have begun to read confidently alone.

humour

humour

Published by Corgi, 1998
ISBN 0-552-54601-1
Illustrations © Tony Ross, 1998

Dogbird by Paul Stewart

Corgi Pups are perfect for new readers just starting to read their own stories. Like most of the titles included in this guide, they share common characteristics of books geared towards children aged six and up; well spaced text in large print combined with plenty of illustrations.

For her seventh birthday Alice chooses a budgie for a present after finding good reasons to rule out a kitten, a guinea pig and even a snake. However, this budgie is not like any other. This budgie doesn't talk, it barks. A barking budgie is bad enough but with three labradors joining in, it's no joke. Trust Alice to end up with a budgie that could only speak *dog*.

With the help of her friend Katie, Alice makes a brave decision to set Dogbird free but not until he finds a home with Grandma is the problem of the barking budgie resolved.

Help! It's Harriet by Jean Ure

Harriet has a good heart and means well, but when she goes to help out, disaster will inevitably strike. Children will love this hilarious story of Harriet's extremely entertaining escapades.

Divided into four chapters with a considerable amount of text, children will feel that they are really mastering the art of independent reading with this book. *Help! It's Harriet* is a **Collins Red Storybook**. Stories in the series are designed for confident young readers.

Published by Collins Children's Books, 1995
ISBN 0-00-675033-8
Illustrations © Stephen Lee, 1995

Published by Walker Books Ltd., 1995
ISBN 0-7445-3666-9
Illustrations © Josip Lizatovic

Beware the Killer Coat by Susan Gates

When Andrew's Mum sees a shiny red coat for sale at bargain price in the second-hand shop, she buys it immediately. Andrew, however, wants a new coat and is convinced that Mum's bargain buy is scowling and snarling at him with its zips like lips of metal teeth.

Andrew's not even surprised when the killer coat traps him inside its darkness, and clings round his face like an octopus while he tries frantically to take it off. The coat loves to eat important school notes, new gloves and it even eats Andrews' pet rat! Will Andrew be able to find a way to defeat the monster coat before he, too, is eaten?

A simple but challenging vocabulary presented in large type makes this story ideal for beginners. Comical drawings and comic-style speech bubbles will attract and hold the interest of reluctant readers.

Dad on the Run by Sarah Garland

Dad on the Run is a story in the **Colour Jets** series. For children who are beginning to read alone this series will certainly appeal, with its humourous stories, full colour illustrations and a mixture of traditional and comic-style text.

Beano's dad, Mr Baxter, has a bad start to his day but it gets worse as the day goes on.
He is wearing his pyjamas, Mrs Baxter's high heeled slippers, his car has been taken by his neighbour, he is miles from home and trying to hide out in Beano's school.

Surely things will improve? Or perhaps he should have stayed in bed.

Published by A&C Black Ltd., 1995
ISBN 0-7136-4186-X
Illustrations © Sarah Garland, 1995

The Dinosaur's Packed Lunch by Jacqueline Wilson

Jacqueline Wilson is a best-selling author for children. Her books for children and teenagers deal sensitively with their everyday problems. In *The Dinosaur's Packed Lunch* Dinah changes from being the little girl without a packed lunch on a school trip to the museum, to being everyone's best friend when she becomes a dinosaur.

Judy who usually sat next to Dinah on the bus sits with Danielle on the trip to the museum and goes off arm in arm with her towards the entrance. She sometimes shared her lunch with Dinah but offers half her Kit Kat bar to Danielle instead today.

Dinah doesn't care because she knows that none of the other children has shared a dinosaur's packed lunch. Even when she has no money to buy stickers and little rubber dinosaurs in the gift shop on the way out, she doesn't mind, happy in the knowledge that no-one else has had a lunch like hers.

Published by Corgi Pups, 1996
ISBN 0-552-52818-8
Illustrations © Nick Sharratt, 1995

Dinah's lunch is not all that's strange; things get even more surprising after she's had a night's sleep.

This is a school story of pure fantasy mixed with real issues as well. Available in the **Corgi Pups** series, it is a perfect book for beginner readers and is much enhanced by the drawings of Nick Sharratt that are instantly recognisable to all readers of Jacqueline Wilson.

A Present from Egypt by Stephanie Baudet

This is the perfect book for a six year old child who wants to read his or her own story, as are other titles in the **Goldcrest** series published by Poolbeg. Young readers will be encouraged by four or five lines of well-spaced text on the first page, which is two-thirds illustration.

The Post Office van arrives with another most peculiar present from Sam's Uncle Max in Egypt. It's a camel. He had previously sent them a rickshaw from China.

The camel, christened Sybil by Sam's mum, provides practical solutions to everyday problems. She even saves the day when Mr Longshanks - the stilt-walker and the star attraction for the fete - breaks his leg and can't lead the procession. Sybil automatically takes his place, just as she takes the place of the family car when it won't start, and takes Sam and his Dad to school and work.

Surprise and humour portrayed by both words and pictures will sustain the young reader's interest throughout the story.

Published by Poolbeg Press Ltd., 1999
ISBN 1-85371- 960- 9
Illustrations © Stewart Curry, 1999

Published by The O'Brien Press Ltd., 2001
ISBN 0-86278-705-X
Illustrations © Conor McHale, 2001

Don't Open That Box! by Conor McHale

A crocodile has escaped from the zoo and is posting himself to unsuspecting people all over the country and eating them on his arrival! It's up to Belzoni the cat and Greta the chicken to outwit the hungry crocodile.

An O'Brien Press **Flyers** book, *Don't Open That Box!* takes young readers on to the next level of reading. Almost identical to the **Panda** series, **Flyers** are a more challenging read for children who have mastered reading alone. The progression from one series to the next will ensure confident reading, without the children themselves even being aware of the development.

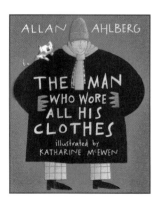

The Man Who Wore All His Clothes by Allan Ahlberg

This is the first story in a series about the most unusual adventures of the Gaskitt family. Mr Gaskitt wears all his clothes at once. Mrs Gaskitt is a taxi driver who, on this occasion, picks up a robber. Gus and Gloria, the twins, have teacher trouble while Horace, the cat, likes easy chairs, old movies on TV and cat food ads.

The robber in Mrs Gaskitt's car somehow or other pulls the many unusual strands of the story together. Mr Gaskitt, wearing all this clothes, saves the day by eventually sitting on the robber and his enormous bag.

Published by Walker Books Ltd., 2002
ISBN 0-7445-8995-9
Illustrations © Katharine McEwen, 2001

For other fun-filled Gaskitt adventures, look out for *The Woman Who Won Things* and *The Cat Who Got Carried Away*.

All three books in the series share charming colour illustrations by Katharine McEwen and large-type text on a white background.

The Man Who Wore All His Clothes has been reviewed by The Independent on Sunday as "Huge fun and ideal for early readers."

Loudmouth Louis by Anne Fine

Louis Todd is the world's greatest expert in being told to be quiet. Louis is a loudmouth. He cannot stay quiet for thirty seconds and is constantly in trouble for talking in class.

When Dad wishes both Louis and Gran would stop talking to allow him watch his football videos in peace and quiet, Louis' idea to raise money for the new school library is born. He decides to hold a sponsored silence for one day. No one believes he can do it but, with the help of his new coach, (his mum), he is determined to become a fly on the wall.

Published by The Penguin Group, 1998
ISBN 0-141-30205-4
Illustrations © Kate Aldous, 1998

stories out of school

Published by The Penguin Group, 1993
ISBN 0-140-36930-9
Illustrations © Julie Douglas, 1996

How to be Cool in Junior School by Betsy Duffey

Young readers will empathise with Robert York and his anxieties on the night before he enters third year in school. He is totally preoccupied with what's cool in junior school. Deciding to change his name must be the first step in the right direction.

Other definite changes include wearing jeans instead of the scratchy new brown shorts laid out carefully by Mother, and her taking pictures of him at the bus stop is now a definite NO.

After his encounter with the habitual bully of school stories, Robbies's refrain "It was going to be a great year!" changes. How to be cool at Junior School is replaced with desperate plans on how to survive it.

Real emotions of growing up are compassionately dealt with by the author who also presents a humourous side to the trials of Robbie.

Going Potty by Eoin Colfer

Ed Cooper is a big boy now and has gone into first class. He has to use the "big boys" toilets now, but he can't. He's afraid of the big toilet. He's also afraid that the big boys might come in because there isn't a lock on the door.

Ed doesn't like to talk about the toilet to anyone, but he writes a letter to his Gran outlining his worries. With the help of Gran's extraordinary potty they find a solution to his problems.

Going Potty deals with a young child's fears and anxieties in school; fear of change, fear of being bullied or laughed at, and anxiety about new teachers. The story is from the **Flyers** series promoted by O'Brien Press as "the second step in reading."

Published by The O'Brien Press Ltd., 1999
ISBN 0-86278-602-9

Pandemonium at School by Jeremy Strong

Seven easy-to-read chapters chart the adventures of Miss Pandemonium from her arrival at Dullandon Primary School to replace Mr. David.

Miss Pandemonium is every child's dream teacher. She is also every Headmaster's worst nightmare. The early chapters tell of the Headmaster's attempts to find a replacement for her, all of which are foiled by Mrs Bunt, the school secretary whose life has become much more enjoyable since Miss Pandemonium joined the staff.

Within a week of her arrival the children spend their classes trying to fly home-made helicopters and making a Friendship Cake, which incidentally becomes a bit too friendly.

These and many other funny exploits of a teacher, who fails to understand how a headmaster can allow life be ruled by a timetable, will keep children entertained to the end.

Published by The Penguin Group, 1999
ISBN 0-141-30495-2
Illustrations © Judy Brown, 1990

Orla at School by Mary Beckett

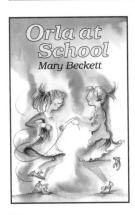

Published by Poolbeg Press Ltd., 1991
ISBN 1-85371-157-8

Orla O'Neill the heroine of Mary Beckett's previous book *Orla is Six* is now aged eight. She still lives in North Belfast and is still teased by her two brothers, Hugh and Art.

The subject of the opening chapter of the book is something that all eight year old girls will understand _ her wish to have a solo part in the school concert. According to Orla's teacher, the most important prerequisite for a solo part is "to behave". When Orla, who always behaves and who so wanted to sing solo, is finally asked, not a single sound comes out.

Similarly when it comes to the school outing, eight year olds will identify with Orla's concerns, like where and when to eat, and who to sit with on the bus.

Other concerns common to Orla and readers of her story include having to keep a friend's secret when she knows she's doing something wrong, and the hurt she feels when her best friend chooses another girl to be friendly with.

The story is divided into five chapters, written in large print. Pencil-line illustrations break up the text at four or five page intervals, providing a reward or diversion for the reluctant reader.

Bobby the Bad by Dick King-Smith

Bobby the Bad is a more challenging read suited to children aged 8 or 9. Bobby Piff is the bad boy in the class who is constantly in trouble with his teacher, Miss Fox. When he unintentionally shoots the Headmaster squarely in the chest with the patent Piff high-explosive imitation-blood bullet, it's no wonder he becomes enemy number one and has his catapult confiscated.

Bobby is every teacher's nightmare; he is rude and insulting and he loves practical jokes, going so far as to superglue Miss Fox to the chair.

But even Bobby can change, with a little help from the bearded educational psychologist, or the man with the upside-down face as Bobby prefers to think of him.
Miss Fox even begins to look forward to his arrival each morning, instead of dreading it.

By the end of the story the reader wonders is he really deserving of the name "Bobby the Bad".

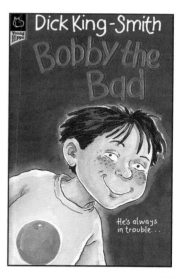

Published by Scholastic Ltd., 1995
ISBN 0-590-13278-4

Bill's New Frock by Anne Fine

When Bill Simpson wakes up one morning his mother dresses him in a pink frock with lovely shell buttons. He goes to school in his frock to find that being a girl has its advantages and disadvantages, and he is amazed at the different way that girls and boys are treated both by adults and their peers.

Mean Malcolm, the school bully whistles at him, instead of kicking him, and he doesn't get picked to carry a table to the nursery room _ not being considered one of the big strong volunteers required.

His work is suddenly supposed to be much neater than the work handed up by the boys and he gets to play the Lovely Rapunzel in class.

Luckily for Bill, by the time he gets home his frock is so dirty that his mother decides it's the last time she will ever send him to school in a frock.

Bill's New Frock won the 1989 Smarties prize for six to eight year olds.

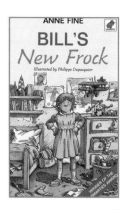

Published by Mammoth Books, 1990
ISBN 0 7497 0305 9
Illustrations © Philippe Dupasquier, 1989

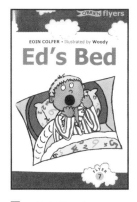

Published by The O'Brien Press Ltd., 2001
ISBN 0-86278-679-7

Ed's Bed by Eoin Colfer

Ed Cooper is an absolute star. He can do everything: read third-class books, spell "tyrannosaurus" and do forward and backward rolls.

But when Ed goes into first class, tables come along. Poor Ed even tries to sneak his table book into bed in an effort to learn his two plusses. Then, to make matters worse, Ed is faced with an even bigger problem of bed wetting. His brilliant plan of hiding a wet sheet in the cistern only leads to further disaster. This story should inspire children to share their worries. Ed realises things aren't quite so bad when three brains, Mum's, Dad's and his own, are working on the problem.

Ed's Bed is Number 7 in the O'Brien **Flyers** series and is aimed at confident readers who can take on longer stories. Slightly more challenging but very similar in format to the **Panda** series, **Flyers** come with plenty of comic-style illustrations, text in large font and bold print and most importantly, first-class stories for early readers.

Conor's Cowboy Suit by Gillian Perdue

The day Conor got a present of a cowboy suit was the best day ever. Conor just loves cowboys, the clothes they wear, their big boots with spurs sticking out the back, and best of all, their gunbelts with two holsters for their shiny guns.

His older sister, Laura, who begs him not to go to school in his cowboy suit, has to admit that Conor is in fact "a cool dude". Not only does he create an opportunity for his own class to dress up every Friday, but Laura's class are going to do the same.

Schoolmates can be cruel at times, but Conor's story subtly illustrates that dressing differently can be a brave and fun thing to do.

Published by The O'Brien Press Ltd., 2002
ISBN 0-86278-778-5

Published by Corgi Pups Books, 1998
ISBN 0-552-54551-1
Illustrations © Peter Kavanagh, 1998

The Frankenstein Teacher by Tony Bradman

Five short chapters tell the spooky story of Class Three's new teacher with comic-style writing and hilarious drawings. While written in simple language there is a huge variety of interesting vocabulary used to tell the story of the Frankenstein teacher.

After the initial shock experienced by all the children on the entrance of the new teacher, things get back to normal pretty quickly and, children being children, resume their frenzied hunt for the missing school hamster.

When the Frankenstein teacher brings the dead hamster back to life the children realise that looks don't really matter. Hannibal the hamster might look a bit different.....! but the ugly Mr. Frankenstein is, without doubt, the best teacher in the world.

Published by Mammoth Books, 1996
ISBN 0-7497-2023-9
Illustrations © Philippe Dupasquier, 1996

How to Write Really Badly by Anne Fine

How to Write Really Badly is another great read from Anne Fine with the usual characteristics of humour, a good storyline and the author's amazing ability to write so appropriately for her readers.

When Chester Howard, an American boy, arrives in Miss Tate's class he finds his jokes are wasted on his new classmates and he begins to wonder if Miss Tate is indeed another "dim-bulb" like the children she teaches in Walbottle Manor (Mixed).

If you dislike school, and teachers even more, and enjoy a good helping of sarcasm, then this is the book for you. Even on the first day the "sheer bloodcurdling niceness" of Chester's classmates defeats him.

Howard, as he has mysteriously come to be known, discovers that Joe who sits next to him can't write a single word properly but he can make a very impressive three-metre model of the Eiffel Tower from macaroni.

Inadvertently Chester involves himself in the education of Joe and when he's asked by Miss Tate to begin his "How To" project, he chooses to provide a how-to manual for poor Joe to finish his school sentence at Walbottle Manor (Mixed).

Chester is completely bowled over when he wins the prize for Most Helpful Person in the class. Winning that prize in Walbottle Manor (Mixed) was, according to Chester, like winning an Olympic Gold. After all these kids were good and nice and kind!

Pandemonium at School Orla at School Bobby the Bad How to Write Really Badly Bill's New Frock Ed's Bed

science fiction

fiction

science fiction & fantasy

& fantasy

Published by The Penguin Group, 1971
ISBN 0-14-030493-2
Illustrations © Hodder & Stoughton Ltd., 1969

A Gift from Winklesea by Helen Cresswell

There's something different about the present that Dan and Mary find in the seaside gift shop for their mother. It is an egg-shaped, bluish-green stone which takes pride of place on the mantelpiece.

Only Mary noticed that the egg-shaped stone always felt warm to touch, almost as if it were going to hatch out. And then one day it did!

Even Dan, after refusing point blank to believe the stone was anything other than a stone, had to admit it had a strange, almost living warmth. Eventually the gift becomes one of the family, living in an aquarium in the kitchen, eating chips and drinking milk, and when the Kane family enter him in the church bazaar pet competition he earns more money than the vicar could ever have hoped for as people queue up to pay to see him.

Helen Cresswell evokes a strange and magical world in a story full of suspense which will encourage the young reader to read it right through to the end.

Bella's Dragon by Chris Powling

Readers will find themselves in the middle of this story straightaway. There is no lead-up or background to the appearance of the dragon in Bella's back garden. Ordinary events, like Bella's day off school because of burst pipes, are presented alongside the extraordinary arrival of a dragon in the garden in a way that reads quite natural.

When Bella tells the dragon to take no notice of inquisitive passers-by, the dragon replies, "I thought they were pointing at you."

This is an example of the consistent humour present throughout the story. Large type with illustrations on every double-page spread and repeated text throughout this **Puffin Read Alone** will appeal to beginner readers.

Published by The Penguin Group, 1990
ISBN 0-14-032735-5
Illustrations © Robert Bartelt, 1990

Aliens Stole My Dog by Ian Whybrow

David finds a CD-ROM in school and decides to bring it home for the weekend to play with it. He gets more of a game than he bargained for when aliens land in his back yard and steal his dog, his teacher and the lollipop lady. David shows the aliens how to have some fun and even manages to get Hairy Spice, the dog back.

A **Books for Boys** logo on the front cover of all books in this series is sure to attract hesitant young male readers.

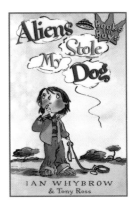

Published by Hodder Children's Books, 2000
ISBN 0-340-77893-8
Illustrations © Tony Ross

The Vegetarian Werewolf by Colin Fletcher

Why does everyone treat Tom like a baby just because he's a bit little? He can't even prove to everyone how good he is at football because everyone says he's too weedy.

Tom proves just how tough he is when he invites a visiting werewolf into his bedroom. Mind you, this is not an ordinary werewolf; he's a werewolf who wished he wasn't!

A lot of people are in for a lot of surprises when Tom puts his brilliant plan of changing places with the werewolf into action. He becomes the winner goal-scoring hero in the schools final and the werewolf, who incidentally is a vegetarian, falls in love and lives happily ever after.

Published by Poolbeg Press Ltd., 2002
ISBN 1-84223-021-2

Spacebaby by Henrietta Branford

When Tipperary and her dog Hector find a baby on the mountain, they take him in and care for him. Tipperary intends taking him to the police to find his parents.

But as the title suggests, Spacebaby is no ordinary baby. He can talk to humans and animals and has come with a mission; to fix the earth's gravity problem. Everything's falling up instead of down!
Full of fantasy, fun and the most unusual characters this is a highly entertaining and exciting story for confident readers.

Published by Collins, 1997
ISBN 0-00-675175-X
Illustrations © Ellis Nadler, 1996

Mona the Vampire and the Tinned Poltergeist by Hiawyn Oram

Published by Orchard Books, 1996
ISBN 1-85213-994-3
Illustrations © Sonia Holleyman, 1996

Children will love the illustrations in this book right through from the title page to the contents, to the detailed map of Columbus Close and the comic drawings of the characters in the book. Mona the Vampire is alerted to something that moves things about and makes people screech by her friend Charley-Knees, alias Zapman.

When Zapman's enterprising brother sets up a stall at the School fair selling screechy, scary things and a tinned poltergeist, "completely real and freshly trapped," Mona is beside herself with rage.

Well-spaced text with illustrations on every page make the book an ideal read for children who have decided to go it alone and who also like a good helping of humour and fantasy.

If you enjoy this story why not read about the further exploits of Mona the Vampire in;
Mona the Vampire and the Big Brown Bap Monster, Mona the Vampire and the Hairy Hands and Mona the Vampire and the Jackpot Disaster.

Fishbum and Splat by Conor McHale

Fishbum and Splat is Conor McHale's third book in the **Flyers** series by O'Brien Press.

The book begins with two little demons from Hell sitting stargazing from their favourite spot: the top of a broken TV set that fell through the roof. But star-gazing is BAD for demons. Curiosity gets the better of them when demon-bait is dropped through the hole in their roof in the shape of an ice-cube, and consequently their journey to Heaven begins.

Read about their unusual adventures and discover why so much broken furniture ends up in their cosy little corner of Hell.

Published by The O'Brien Press Ltd., 2001
ISBN 0-86278-735-1

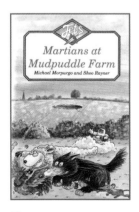

Published by Collins 1993
ISBN 0-00-674494-X
Illustrations © Shoo Rayner, 1992

Martians at Mudpuddle Farm by Michael Morpurgo

Martians at Mudpuddle Farm is a story about animals with a good helping of the supernatural thrown in to capture the imagination of children as young as six. Lots of illustration, comic-style text and an amusing story written in large type are characteristics of the **Jets** series.

Little Bee getting lost and requiring the whole swarm to search for her could mean Farmer Rafferty will never earn the honey money he needs to buy a new tractor. However a series of events lead to the farm opening to the public; the main attraction being a perfect corn circle that Farmer Rafferty thinks is the work of Martians with ray guns. Only the animals know what really happened!

Intergalactic Kitchen   A Gift from Winklesea   Bella's Dragon   Aliens Stole My Dog   The Vegetarian Werewolf

Dracula's Daughter by Mary Hoffman

First published in 1988, this title in the **Yellow Bananas** series has been reprinted several times. Banana Books are synonymous with early reading and are now divided into colour-coded series to match ability. Mary Hoffman has written countless books for children including picture books and books for teenage readers.

In *Dracula's Daughter* Mr. and Mrs. Batty are delighted to welcome into their lives the abandoned baby girl found on their doorstep. Only when she reaches the age of five, and with the onset of her second teeth, do they begin to wonder why she has grown fangs. Doesn't it seem strange that she enjoys all sorts of meat that other children usually refuse to eat?

Like all **Banana Books**, *Dracula's Daughter* is beautifully illustrated throughout with full colour pictures.

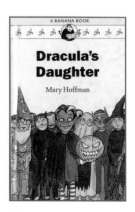

Published by Heinemann, 1988
ISBN 0-434-93048-2
Illustrations © Chris Riddell, 1988

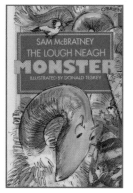

Published by The O'Brien Press Ltd., 1994
ISBN 0-86278-375-5

The Lough Neagh Monster by Sam McBratney

Nessie the Lough Ness monster is full of mischief and is sometimes a downright pest. She loves to play games and frighten people. She goes to Lough Neagh to visit her cousin Noblett, a very well behaved monster, and gets into all kinds of trouble.

How is Noblett going to get his life back to normal and get rid of his trouble-making cousin?

Now published in the **Flyers** series with characteristic illustrated text, *The Lough Neagh Monster* is suitable for children who can read confidently alone.

The Origami Bird by Lorraine Francis

The origami bird's home is the classroom windowsill. With the help of a wren and a robin he finds out what it's like to be a real bird, flying high in the sky, building a nest and feeding the baby birds.

An interesting subject is introduced in this - a simple story for young children - enhanced by the illustrations of Anne O'Hara. Instructions on how to make an origami bird on the last page is an additional appealing feature.

The Origami Bird is a **Goldcrest Reader** from Poolbeg Press. All titles in the series are ideally suited to beginner readers.

Published by Poolbeg Press Ltd., 2001
ISBN 1-84223-019-0

The Intergalactic Kitchen by Frank Rodgers

Published by The Penguin Group, 1991
ISBN 0-14-036400-5
Illustrations © Frank Rodgers, 1990

An ideal mix of standard text and comic strip add to this highly entertaining, fantasy story for beginner readers.

In the first book in the intergalactic kitchen series about the Bird family, Mr Bird works in the secret BONCE (National Bureau of Clever Experts) establishment.

He installs a high tech protection system to take care of his family should the most serious class 1A emergency strike, and of course it does.

Following her husband's instructions, Mrs. Bird and her children blast off into space in the family kitchen. Mrs. Bird gets her much-yearned for holiday in the sun after all, without the help of the travel agents. After all who needs travel agents when their house is equipped with an intergalactic kitchen!

leabhair
gaeilge

leabhair gaeilge

Tá na leabhair seo go léir foilsithe ag Preas O' Brien agus an Gúm. Tá na leabhair ata foilsithe ag O'Brien sa sraith SOS agus tá roinnt dóibh ar fáil as Bearla sa sraith O'Brien Panda.

Tá na teidil seo feiliúnach mar bhuntús do paisti óga mar tá léaráidí greannmhara, téamaí tarraingteacha agus téacs so- léite iontu. Is acmhainn iontacha iad do thuismitheoirí scéalta as Ghaeilge a bheith ar fáil do páisti de cúig nó sé bliana d'aois.

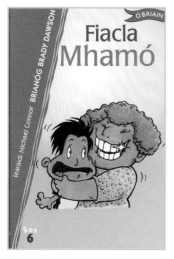

Foilsithe ag Cló Uí Bhriain Teo., 2001
ISBN 0-86278-741-6

Fiacla Mhamó le Brianóg Brady Dawson

Cá bhfuil fiacla Mhamo? Tá siad i mála scoile Danny. Bhí sport iontach ag Danny leis na fiacla ar scoil. Ach féach cad a tharla nuair a tháinig sé abhaile!

An Leaba Sciathánach le Áine Ní Ghlinn

Bhí ionadh an domhain ar Niall agus Teidí nuair a thosaigh a leaba ag bogadh agus iad ag iarraidh dul a chodladh. Ach ansin fásann sciatháin as an leaba agus suas san aer leí de phreab !

Dúirt Teidí go raibh siad ag dul go Pláinéad na mBéar ansin, rud a chuir ionadh orthu go léir. Bhí scanradh an domhain ar Niall i dtosach ach tar éis tamaill thosaigh sé ag baint an taitneamh as an Pláinéad nua agus bhí cuid mhór spraoi acu ann.

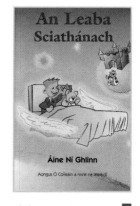

Foilsithe ag An Gúm, 2001
ISBN 1-85791-413-9

Foilsithe ag Cló Uí Bhriain Teo., 2001
ISBN 0-86278-724-6

Sailí na Spotaí le Anne Marie Herron

Is breá le Sailí spotaí. Spotaí ar a cuid éadaigh, spotaí ar a cuid bréagán, spotaí ar gach rud! Ní éireoidh Sailí tuirseach de na spotaí go deo - nó an éireoidh?

An Camán Draíochta le Brian de Bhaldraithe

Tá Scoil Dhara i gcluiche ceannais an Choirn den chéad uair riamh. Cúpla lá roimh an gcluiche mór tagann Cian de thaisme ar sheanchamán. Tuigeann sé ón gcéad uair a thógann sé ina lámh é gur dó féin a rinneadh é.

Foilsithe ag An Gúm, 2002
ISBN 1-85791-240-3

Moncaí Dána le Áine Ní Ghlinn

Is moncaí dána é Colm. "Ú-ú-ú!" a deir sé arís is arís eile. Bíonn cóisir aisteach aige - an aisteach!
Ní chreidfidh tú cad a tharlaíonn do Cholm agus dá chairde!

Foilsithe ag Cló Uí Bhriain Teo., 2002
ISBN 0-86278-790-4

Bróga Thomáis le Úna Leavy

Ní chaitheann Tomás bróga, ni maith leis bróga ar chor ar bith; ní chaitheann sé fiú amháin stocaí. Bíonn Mamaí agus Dadaí i gconaí ag iarraidh bróga a chur ar Thomás, ach teipeann orthú i gconaí.

Tugann Deaidí Tomás go dtí an siopa bróg agus taispeánann fear an tsiopa gach saghas bróg dó Thomáis, ach fós níl suim ar bith ag Tomás bróga a chaitheamh.

Ach lá amháin tosnaíonn sé ag cur sneachta agus téann Tomás amach chun spraoi ann.Tar éis tamaill bíonn a chosa beaga chomh fuar agus reoite go mbíonn air dul abhaile agus fanacht istigh. Tá bronnantas ag Mamaí dó anois a réitíonn na fadhbanna go léir; céard atá ann?

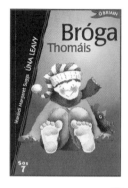

Foilsithe ag Cló Uí Bhriain Teo., 2002
ISBN 0-86278-782-3

Foilsithe ag Cló Uí Bhriain Teo., 2001
ISBN 0-86278-713-0

Deirdre agus an Fear Bréige le Úna Leavy

Bhí sceitiminí an domhain ar Deirdre nuair a fuair sí an pháirt mar Bhanríon sa dráma ar scoil.

Thug Mamaí agus Daidí cabhair di coróin na banríona a dhéanamh. Le gliú, cairtchlár péint agus tinsil rinne Mamaí, Dadaí agus Deirdre an choróin is áille a bhfaca siad riamh.

D'fhág Deirdre an choróin ar an bhfuinneog sa chistin ansin agus suas an staighre lei chun dul a codladh.

Ach cá bhfuil an choróin ar maidin?

Mise agus mo Mhamó le Beartla Ó Brádaigh

Is iontach go deo an Mhamó atá ag an ngasúr óg sa leabhar seo.

Téann sé ar cuairt chuichi gach Domhnach agus déanann sí cístí beaga dó a mbíonn an- bhlasta ar fad. Tugann sí folcadh do na páisí óga, agus bíonn sí go minic ag obair sa ghairdín, rud is aoibheann leo go léir.

Is iontach an duine í Mamó.

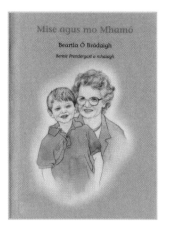

Foilsithe ag An Gúm, 2001
ISBN 1-85791-205-5

Foilsithe ag Cló Uí Bhriain Teo., 2001
ISBN 0-86278-712-2

Cáitín sa Chistin le Stephanie Dagg

Lá Breithlá Aintín Síle a bhí ann agus rinne Mamaí cáca deas mór. Bhí gach saghas reoán ar an gcáca, reoán buí, reoán dearg agus reoán glas agus cheap Cáitín agus Mamaí gurbh é an cáca is deise riamh a bhí ann.

D'fhág Mamaí an cáca sa chistin agus chuaigh sí ag féachaint ar an teilifís. "Ná bain leis an gcáca sin", arsa Mamaí do Cháitín agus í ag imeacht.

Ach thosaigh Caitín ag ithe an reón píosa i ndiaidh píosa- ní raibh sí ábalta stop a chur leí féin . Tar éis tamaill bhí an reón ar fad imithe agus bhí an cáca scroiste. Beidh fearg an domhain ar Mamaí,

Ach tá plean maith ag Cáitín, bheul cheap sí gur plean maith é ar aon nós. Ach tá tuairimí difriúila ag Mamaí.

Sciathánach Sailí na Spotaí Fiacla Mhamó An Camán Draíochta Moncaí Dána Bróga Thomáis Deirdre agus an

Céard atá sa Bhosca le Áine Ní Ghlinn

Bhí sceitiminí an domhain ar Sheán ag dul ar scoil Dé Luain. Bhí bosca mór ina láimh aige.
"Céard atá sa bhosca ? arsa Mamaí. "Caithfaidh tú fanacht le fáil amach" a deir Seán. Bhí scanradh ar a dheirfiúr Síle mar cheap sí go raibh damhán alla nó rud éigin gránna sa bhosca aige.

Ar an mbealach go dtí an scoil, stop a chairde é ag iarraidh fáil amach céard a bhí i dtaisce aige sa bhosca, agus ar scoil ní raibh éinne sa rang in ann aon obair a dhéanamh le teann fiosrachta : bhí siad go léir ag iarraidh fáil amach céard a bhí sa bhosca.

Ach an raibh siad sásta sa deireadh nuair a d'oscail Seán an bhosca ?

Foilsithe ag An Gúm, 2002
ISBN 1-85791-457-0

Daifní Dineasár le Áine Ní Ghlinn

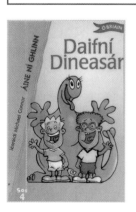

Is breá le Conall agus Niall cleasanna a imirt, go háraithe ar Mhamaí. Bíonn siad i gconaí ag spraoi agus ag insint scéalta do Mhamaí.

Ach céard a tharlaíonn nuair a thugann Daifní Dineasár cuairt ag an teach nuair atá Conall agus Niall ag an pictiúrlann le Mamó ?

Cé atá sa seomra codlata nuair a théann na páisti suas staighre? Ach an creideann Mamaí iad???.

Foilsithe ag Cló Uí Bhriain Teo., 2001
ISBN 0-86278-745-9

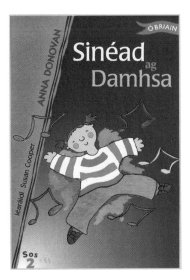

Foilsithe ag Cló Uí Bhriain Teo., 2001
ISBN 0-86278-714-9

Sinéad ag Damhsa le Anna Donovan

Is breá le Sinéad a bheith ag damhsa, bíonn sí i gconaí ag léim, ag scoirr, agus ag casadh a lámha timpeall is timpeall san aer. Bhí sceitiminí an domhain uirthí nuair a duairt a máthair go raibh cead aici dul go rang damhsa.

Thosaigh sí ag dul go rang damhsa Gaelach. Bhí fearg ar an muinteóir Gaelach áfach nuair a thosaigh Sinéad ar a stíl féin. Duairt an múinteoir ba cheart dí dul go rang Bailé.

Ach ní raibh Sinéad ró shásta nuair a duairt an muinteoir Bailé go gcathfaidh sí seasamh direach lena lámha thuas san aer. Duairt si freisin nach mbeidh Sinéad riamh ina damhsóir Bailé, agus ba cheart dí dul go rang gleacaíochta.

Faoi dheireadh an bhfuil an rang ceart faighte ag Sinéad? An feidir lei a stíl féin a dhéanamh?

Also available from Clare County Library

Picture This!
A Guide to Choosing Books for Young Children

Published by Clare County Library, 2002
ISBN 0 9541870 0 8

Price €9.00

The following review of *Picture This!* appeared in *Books Ireland* magazine, May 2002

"With an introduction by Clare County Librarian, Noel Crowley, and a foreword by children's author Siobhan Parkinson, this is an extremely attractively produced guide to some eighty picture books.

Each book's jacket is reproduced in full colour and each title is given a review of some sixty words. Parents, teachers and all concerned with finding colourful, stimulating and engaging reading material with which to delight their young acquaintances will find regular use for this equally colourful, stimulating and engaging guide.

'Lavish' is the only word for this very well-produced guide, in which book covers are reproduced in full colour and occupying a whole page apiece with comments on each book and its target readership."